*f***P**

Scott W. Ventrella

THE POWER OF POSITIVE THINKING IN BUSINESS

•

*Ten Traits for
Maximum Results*

THE FREE PRESS

NEW YORK LONDON TORONTO SYDNEY SINGAPORE

*ƒ*P
THE FREE PRESS
A Division of Simon & Schuster Inc.
1230 Avenue of the Americas
New York, NY 10020

Copyright © 2001 by Scott W. Ventrella and the Peale Center

THE FREE PRESS and colophon are trademarks
of Simon & Schuster Inc.

Designed by Karolina Harris

Manufactured in the United States of America

10   9   8   7   6   5   4   3   2   1

Library of Congress Cataloging-in-Publication Data
Ventrella, Scott W.
   The power of positive thinking in business : ten traits for
maximum results / Scott W. Ventrella.
      p.   cm.
   Based on Norman Vincent Peale's The power of positive thinking.
   1. Business—Religious aspects—Christianity.   2. Success in business.
3. Success—Religious aspects—Christianity.   4. Peace of mind—Religious
aspects—Christianity.   I. Peale, Norman Vincent, 1898–1993—Power of
positive thinking.   II. Title.

HF5388. V46 2001
650.1—dc21

                                                           00-52821

ISBN 0-7432-1237-1

To my wife, Catherine,
and our two precious children,
Jennifer and Andrew

Contents

PART THREE: THE ENERGIZING POWER

Foreword:
The Legacy

It was my husband's insight that we are all born positive thinkers but some of the traits of positive thinking have become clouded over by the inevitable stresses of our daily lives.

Norman spent much of his professional life showing people how to recapture their innate positiveness, especially when faced with adversity or challenge.

Norman wanted to bring positive thinking to the business community because business has a tremendous influence on our lives and our culture. Because the rapidity of change in the workplace today is greater than ever, it is especially important for business-people to be equipped to meet that challenge with methodologies to manage change. In this sense, *The Power of Positive Thinking in Business* is a natural extension of Norman's work.

The Power of Positive Thinking in Business is an adaptation of the proven work of Norman Vincent Peale to help you become more effective. In the workplace of the twenty-first century, I am confident you will find it particularly relevant and useful. I hope you enjoy your journey toward becoming a positive-thinking person.

Mrs. Ruth Stafford Peale

Part One

THE CASE FOR POSITIVE THINKING

1

A Winning Program

"Believe in yourself! Have faith in your abilities! Without a humble but reasonable confidence in your own powers you cannot be successful or happy. But with sound self-confidence you can succeed." When I first read those opening lines from Dr. Norman Vincent Peale's best-selling book *The Power of Positive Thinking,* they shook me to the core. The words rang with truth and power, and like millions of others, I became "hooked" on the concepts of positive thinking. And like millions of other people, I adopted the principles in all aspects of my life, which led to an incredible personal transformation. Barely twenty-one years old, I became a new man! My personal relationships improved vastly. I became more confident and focused. The "bad breaks" I had been experiencing seemed to evaporate. And unlike other self-improvement concepts, positive thinking principles stayed with me and led me to many successes in my personal and professional life. Most self-improvement programs are a lot like Chinese food; that is, it tastes great and fills you up, but then a few hours later you're ready for pizza. The principles of positive thinking are different because they are built on a solid foundation of indisputable, universal spiritual and scientific principles. It was while working with the Juran Institute, a quality management consulting firm, that I made the connection between positive thinking and business. During my eleven years with Juran as a consultant, I worked with numerous organizations, helping them to achieve greater levels of performance by focusing on quality.

Much of the emphasis was on making higher-quality goods and services: *things* and the *processes* by which they were created. What bothered me was that little attention was paid to the *people* responsible for making the "things" and designing the processes. What finally convinced me that we were neglecting a critical performance issue was a discussion I had with Ritz-Carlton's CEO, Horst Schulze. Ritz-Carlton had just won the coveted Malcolm Baldrige National Quality Award (MBNQA), which recognizes companies for outstanding quality. It had invested thousands of dollars in learning and applying TQM concepts and practices companywide. I wanted to hear directly from Horst what he thought the key to the company's success was. The "people" factor had been brewing in my head, and I wanted to independently, albeit nonscientifically, corroborate it. I asked him a simple, nonleading question: "Mr. Schulze, of all the business concepts you employed to become an MBNQA winner, which would you say was the single most important factor?" It took him barely ten seconds to respond: "People! Having motivated, energetic, hardworking people with great attitudes. That's the single most important factor." He was not suggesting that it was the only factor but that it was the most critical. As I conducted more formal research on MBNQA winners, the "people factor" emerged as a common denominator of success. Companies such as Motorola, FedEx, Westinghouse, Milliken, Xerox, and others had all made huge investments in developing their people. But which aspects of people development yield the greatest return? Which aspects help us bring out the highest potential of our people?

WHY DO SO MANY PEOPLE FAIL TO REACH THEIR FULL POTENTIAL IN BUSINESS?

In my workshops I ask participants to take a moment and, on a blank sheet of paper, write all the reasons why, in their opinion, people fail to reach their full potential in business. Perhaps you'll want to try it, too. It's important not to read ahead before doing this simple, yet revealing exercise. So go ahead and make your list. Write down as many ideas as you can think of without evaluating them. Once you've created your list, evaluate and place in rank order your top three

---

Limitations to Success
Lack of resources
No management support
Fear
No clear goals
Low self-esteem
Lack of planning
Unorganized
Lack of training
Lack of confidence
Not given adequate time, money, or oppportunity
And so on

---

reasons. I've conducted this exercise hundreds of times with people in all walks of life. Now take a look at the box above. It lists typical responses.

Now review the list. Were any of the responses similar to what appeared on your list? Chances are that many were very similar, if not the same. Do you see a pattern? What many people immediately notice is that the list can be divided into two broad categories, internal and external. Look at the list again (either yours or the one in the book): Which factors are internal, and which are external? For instance, is lack of confidence internal or external? Most people would agree that it is something internal to the individual and therefore more directly controllable than an external factor. How about fear? Low self-esteem? What were your top three reasons? Are they internal or external? More than 95 percent of the time, people list *internal* factors as reasons why people fail to reach their full potential in business. According to the noted psychologist Dr. James Fadiman, "When we get stuck while trying to reach a goal, it usually isn't because we need to learn a new technique. Rather, it's because we've run up against one or more *internal barriers.* Until we deal with those inner obstacles, all the good intentions, plans, and motivational strategies in the world won't be good enough to see us through to our goals."

What we're talking about here is *attitude.* Each year companies invest millions of dollars in knowledge and skills-based training to improve performance. Yet the results have been dismal. In proportion to the investment, little improvement is made, certainly not enough to justify the investment. Training focused on knowledge and skills is not enough. In most cases where people know what to do (that is, they have the knowledge) and how to do it (they have the skills), they still don't follow through (perform) nearly as well as they could. Self-limiting beliefs and negative thoughts that shape attitude are the culprits, blocking effective application of knowledge and skills.

What about the external factors? Are they really outside our control? Can we do anything about "lack of training" or "no management support"? How about "lack of resources"? Of course not; that is, not directly. What we can do is change our *view* of these external factors. In the words of Stoic philosopher Epictetus, "Man is disturbed not by things but the view he takes of those things."

We can choose to allow external factors to defeat us, or we can choose to view them in a hopeful, expectant manner. And when we view external factors in this manner, we find that we really can—and do—have control over them.

External factors affecting performance can be grouped into three "excuse" categories, what I call the "three Ls":

- Lack: Don't have "it," never did, never will.
- Loss: Had "it" but lost it.
- Limitation: Have "it" but in limited quantities.

When we fail to achieve a particular goal or level of success, we often blame it on one of the "three Ls."

An individual with the "lack" mentality is always complaining that he or she doesn't have the resources necessary to be successful: money, education, connections, and so on. Some of us fall back on the "loss" mentality: "Things were going well with my project until two of my team members were reassigned to a new project. I can't possibly finish it in time now." Finally, there's the "limitation" mentality: "I'd like to go for that new position, but I don't have enough experience or education. I'd probably fail." Many people experience one or a combination of the "three Ls," but instead of using it as an excuse, they use it to motivate and mobilize themselves. They realize that the only real inhibitors are the conclusions they reach about external barriers.

Earlier in this chapter, I made a distinction between internal and external barriers to achieving our potential in the workplace. But as you can now see, essentially all barriers are *internal* and therefore can be controlled directly. Is there anything we can do about internal barriers? Before responding, let's review where we are: knowledge and skills, in and of themselves, do not lead to high performance in the workplace. A critical ingredient in the mix is attitude, which, when positive, enables us to overcome our internal barriers. When our attitude is negative, the internal barriers overwhelm and ultimately defeat us. Attitude, by definition, is a "mental position or feeling about an object." If we can change our mental position (thoughts) and feelings, we can change our behavior. But can we really change our thoughts and feelings? As managers, can we change the thoughts and feelings of others? How? Most managers are trained to focus only on results, which are the *consequences* of behavior. People whose behavior leads to good results are rewarded. People whose behaviors do not lead to good results are either not rewarded or are punished and/or sent back to training! Most managers are not comfortable with the idea of changing people's thoughts and feelings. That's the job of an organizational psychologist, isn't it? A manager might argue that the best she can do is hire people with good attitude, and hope that the attitude stays positive.

Of course, we can screen prospective employees and hire on the basis of attitude. Some good assessment tools are available for that purpose. But who doesn't hire for attitude? Some managers believe that employees can be grouped into two categories: those with positive attitudes and those with negative attitudes. But if we hire for only positive attitude, why do so many companies have problems with poor attitude? I remember attending a meeting of human resource professionals who were part of a *Fortune* 100 service company. The meeting was kicked off by the president, who happened to be an advocate of positive thinking. He told the group that the single most important success factor for the organization was attitude. And it was his opinion that "there are too many people in this company with bad attitudes." To my astonishment, he continued by saying, "I think we should find all the people with bad attitudes and fire them!" Although he knew he couldn't really do that, he was dead serious. What he didn't realize is that most people start their jobs with a positive, hopeful outlook. Most people come to work every day earnestly looking to do the best job they can. But as in most areas of life, we are beset with problems, challenges, and crises in the workplace every day. Even the most positive people can be beaten down. The challenge for managers is to create an environment that constantly reinforces and nurtures positive attitudes. Some good managers are inherently effective in this regard. But others require a "road map," so to speak, to show them how. This is where positive thinking plays such a powerful role—because it provides a road map to help people get to the *source* of the internal barriers—negativity, pessimism, poor attitude—that affect performance.

THE ROAD MAP TO POSITIVE THINKING

Most of us can remember a time, whether in our personal or professional lives, when we were faced with a daunting, perhaps life-threatening situation. And most of us can remember handling that tough situation effectively—as a result of positive thinking. The fact is that all of us are positive thinkers to one degree or another. All of us have employed positive thinking techniques to get ourselves out of a jam. Most of the time we *react* to situations and employ positive thinking in an unstructured way. But applying positive thinking in business requires that we develop a more structured, methodical approach to *proactively* dealing with both planned and unplanned challenging situations. The positive thinking road map involves seven steps, which I will outline here briefly. In subsequent chapters, I develop each step in much greater detail.

1. Define the situation.
Successful resolution of a business challenge begins with investing enough time and effort to define it clearly, yet comprehensive. Doing so may take only a few minutes, but this simple act can
- Give you a clear target on which to focus your efforts.
- Lessen any anxiety you may be feeling about the situation.

Most challenging situations in the workplace require an appropriate mix of knowledge, skills, and positive attitudes and behaviors.

This step presumes that you possess the requisite knowledge and skills to tackle a situation. But all situations in business, no matter how simple or complex, require that we interact effectively with other people. In defining the situation, we need to focus on two areas. The first is our view of the situation. The second is the manner in which we conduct ourselves when dealing with other people. The definition of the situation should be a short, concise description of the *business* issue and the emotional gravity of the situation.

Here are some examples:

- My team's attitude and performance are down. I need to turn this situation around, starting with our next meeting. I am worried that we will not accomplish our objectives by year's end.
- I have yet another project deadline to meet, but I'm burning out from a relentless workload. The more I do, the more is handed to me. I am frustrated, anxious, and ready to explode.
- I've just been passed over for a promotion I know I deserve, and I'm going to confront my manager. I am hurt and angry.
- I must give a presentation to management explaining why my project is over budget and overdue. I am fearful and anxious.
- It's performance review time, and I have an employee who thinks his performance was stellar, when in fact it was mediocre. I should have confronted him about this a month ago, but I waited, hoping that things would improve. He's going to be disappointed and potentially confrontational. I'm afraid and really don't want to have to deal with him directly.

A well-defined problem is a problem half solved! To get the most benefit from this book, I suggest that you take few minutes *now* to identify and define a challenging situation you are currently facing or expect to face in the near future. Jot it down on a pad and hold on to it. As you read through the book, there will be other opportunities to continue planning for a successful outcome to your particular challenge, and you will also find a useful guide in the Resource Section at the end of this book.

2. What are you telling yourself?

With regard to the problematic situation you just defined, what are you saying to yourself? As you know, your thoughts about any situation you are facing can work for or against you. Simply put: Think positive, become positive; think negative, become negative. Your self-talk (what you're telling yourself about the situation) is the key to determining whether you're thinking clearly and rationally or letting negative emotions such as anxiety, fear, anger, and frustration get the better of you. Chapters 3 and 4 will explain this concept more fully, as well as a method known as "truth in thinking" that can help you deal more constructively with negative self-talk.

3. What is your desired outcome?

At this point, you should be clear about the situation you're facing and view it in an appropriately positive and constructive light. *Now you're in a position to specify the outcome you desire.* The outcome should be expressed in measurable ways. It should include both quantitative and qualitative measurements. This step combines three powerful concepts:

1. Setting goals
2. Affirmation
3. Visualization

You have a much better chance of getting what you want if you know what you want and can write a plan using the SMART method: Specific, Measurable, Action-oriented, Realistic, and Time-bound.

Once you've set some SMART goals, you'll want to prepare a plan for accomplishing them. The next step will help you do this.

4. Access your positive traits.

Achieving your goals requires that you identify and eliminate negative attitudinal barriers (see step 2). In doing this, you will create a fertile environment for cultivating the positive behaviors inherent in all of us. There are ten specific behavioral traits that are characteristic of a positive-thinking and positive-living person: optimism, enthusiasm, belief, integrity, courage, confidence, determination, patience, calmness, and focus. These traits can be leveraged and brought to bear on challenging situations to help you meet your goals and objectives.

5. Rehearse the situation mentally.

According to a recent *Wall Street Journal* article, today's most successful business executives attribute their success to six activities, mental rehearsal being one of them. As confirmed by many business and sports professionals, by mentally rehearsing every facet and feeling of what needs to happen for you to obtain your desired outcome, you will vastly improve your odds of attaining it.

6. Take action.

After taking the preceding steps, you should be well positioned to take positive action. At this point, it's a good idea to create a plan outlining the specific steps you'll need to take. This is an organic process, not a mechanical one, and you will discover that some challenging situations extend over periods of weeks and months and thus involve numerous substeps. A detailed plan will help you think through how you're going to approach each phase of the situation.

7. Assess the results of your actions.

This is the final step. By taking time to reflect thoughtfully after taking action, you will position yourself for improved performance in the future. With hindsight you'll probably recognize that certain aspects of your performance were very effective, while others were less so. The intent here is for you to invest some time in assessing your action(s) so that in the future you can repeat what works for you and, equally important, correct any shortcomings you may have identified.

You can begin your after-action assessment by asking yourself the following questions:

- To what extent did I attain my desired outcome?
- What went well? Why?
- Which aspects of my plan (Road Map Steps 1–6) were most effective? Why?

- What could have gone better?
- What would I do differently next time?
- What were the specific success ingredients?

The positive thinking road map provides a comprehensive structure for planning, implementing, and evaluating our performance in challenging situations. This structure makes it possible for anybody in an organization to learn and apply positive thinking methods to business challenges with measurable outcomes. As managers, our first responsibility is to apply the road map to our own challenging situations. Next, we can be role models for positive thinking attitudes and behaviors. We also need to coach others using positive thinking tools and techniques. This helps to create and perpetuate a positive culture.

Positive thinking in business has many benefits:
- It is the key to bringing out the potential of all employees, which is the driver for high performance.
- It is the single most important factor for creating outstanding service—just ask the people at the Walt Disney Company or Southwest Airlines!
- It stimulates innovation and creativity.
- It fosters an open, honest, trusting work environment.
- It greatly enhances interpersonal relationships, which are the key to getting things done.
- It saves a great deal of money.

THE POWER OF NEGATIVE THINKING
IN BUSINESS

The cost-saving benefits of positive thinking deserve some extra attention. According to the Bureau of Labor Statistics, U.S. companies lose about $3 billion a year due to negativity. This comes in the form of lost productivity due to gossiping, griping, complaining, and undermining the efforts of others. There are also costs related to customer dissatisfaction and loss of goodwill. Customers experiencing poor service will look for alternatives. If customers' complaints about poor service are met with a bad attitude, it often infuriates them and prompts them to take further action.

One of my client companies has a very fair and equitable grievance process for all its employees. It is designed to provide anyone who feels he was unfairly treated with a means of stating his case to, if necessary, the highest levels within the organization. There are tremendous costs associated with this process, since anybody can initiate it at any time. If the process works its way up two or three levels, it occupies the time of highly paid managers and executives, who ideally should be focusing their attention on other, value-added areas.

I am not suggesting that the grievance process is unnecessary. It plays an important role in the organization and is viewed very positively by employees. I *am* suggesting that use of the grievance process can be greatly reduced by learning how to deal more effectively and fairly with people. By applying positive thinking concepts, my client was able to significantly reduce the number of grievances filed and the amount of time spent on the grievance process.

In another instance, a friend of mine who works in health care encountered some problems with her supervisor. Being a direct, open person, she decided to meet with the supervisor to see if they could identify the source of their disagreements and resolve the issue. Unfortunately, during the meeting the supervisor became defensive and hostile. Other managers were called in, and after considerable intervention the situation was eventually sorted out. Could this situation have been avoided altogether? I believe so. Managers spend an inordinate amount of their time each day dealing with nonproductive, energy-sapping issues resulting from negativity in the workplace.

I've mentioned these examples of "negativity costs" because they're often overlooked and shrugged off as a cost of doing business. But living with, or putting up with, negativity doesn't have to be that way. Changing, or moving toward a positive work environment, all starts with a good understanding of what positive thinking *really* is.

The Meaning of Positive Thinking

Pause for a moment and think about the words "positive thinking." What comes to mind? What words or images do you think of? Are there certain people you can think of whom you consider to be positive thinkers?

Over the years I have asked hundreds, if not thousands, of people from all walks of life what they think of when they hear the words "positive thinking." Here are some of the typical responses I've recorded:

"It's looking on the bright side of situations."
"It's looking at life through rose-colored glasses."
"It's being happy and upbeat."
"It's having an unrealistic view of the world."

Obviously, some of the responses were more positive and others more negative. People with a more negative view are inclined to dismiss the notion of positive thinking out of hand. Interestingly enough, those possessing a more cynical view are sometimes warranted in their thinking. I know of one very reputable organization that, after many years of prosperity, fell on hard times. The CEO of this company, whom I know personally, tried his hardest to put a positive spin on the situation: "Everything's going great—no problem"; "Don't worry, it's just a temporary setback, we'll be back on our feet soon."

Unfortunately, he did little to address some of the critical business issues involved, and as a result the company has slumped deeper and deeper into financial despair, almost to the point of bankruptcy. The problem with the CEO's spin on the situation is that the company really *was* in trouble—and everybody in the organization knew it. But rather than admitting that there was a serious problem, the CEO ignored it. So his "positiveness" was viewed as being insincere and out of touch with reality—and all the while he was thinking he was boosting morale. Should a manager be faulted for trying to stay upbeat during trying times? Unfortunately, the answer is "yes" if that positivity is a smokescreen for inaction. As we shall soon learn, positive thinkers are tough-minded, reality-based people who blast through problems with energy and zeal.

It's important to clear up some of the confusion surrounding people's ideas of positive thinking.

THE POSITIVE THINKING QUIZ

The following quiz will test your own ideas of the meaning of positive thinking. Simply indicate whether you think each statement is true or false. Once you're finished, I'll review each question and provide an explanation of the most accurate response.

1. Negative people are born that way.
2. In most instances, what keeps people from fulfilling their potential is circumstances beyond their control.
3. Self-confidence is something that can be faked.
4. Saying that someone is a positive thinker is the same as saying that he or she is a Pollyanna.
5. Our beliefs shape our behavior, which in turn shapes our feelings.
6. Sometimes you have to ignore facts in order to be a positive thinker.
7. We cannot change the reality of most situations; we can control only our responses to it.
8. Our self-expectations are usually not predictors of achievement.

9. Facts are more important than attitude.
10. If you don't make choices in your life, others will make them for you.

Let's review these.

1. Negative people are born that way.

False. Contrary to what many people think, most negativity is *learned.* Not long ago I was having a discussion with a woman who was interested in participating in a positive thinking workshop. She was intrigued with the idea that positive thinking concepts could be brought into the workplace. She was skeptical about whether or not people can be "taught" to be positive. She provided the following il- lustration: "My husband is a natural-born positive thinker, always was, always will be. On the other hand, I have always been pes- simistic, always was, always will be. Therefore," she went on, "either you have it or you don't, and if you don't, there's nothing you can do about it." She viewed positive thinking as a genetic feature, like being born with brown eyes, and as a result, there's nothing that can be done about it. The fact is that most of us are *born* positive thinkers. Al- though volumes of research support this premise, simple observation usually clears away all doubt.

Have you ever seen a negative baby? Parents with young children know the answer to this: No, of course you don't see negative babies. I remember being awakened early one morning, at 5 A.M., to be exact, by my infant son, Andrew. I recall hearing cooing noises and "sense- less" chatter, as he was too young to form words.

I rose out of bed—or rather, I stumbled out of bed and into his room to see what was going on. I thought perhaps I could reason with him—you know, talk some sense into him to see if he'd be open to the idea of sleeping for a few more hours. The little guy greeted me, the grouch of the East, with the biggest smile you'd ever want to see. If he could've talked at the time, I imagine he would have said some- thing like "Good morning, Dad, isn't it a terrific day? Can you get me out of my crib so we can play, huh, Dad, can you?" Unfortunately for many of us, this natural positive state is not maintained. Due largely to strong influences on us early in life, we move away from our natural positive state and slowly drift into a more unnatural, negative one. Negativity is essentially a learned behavior. Children normally hear the word "no" ten times more than the word "yes." Most of the time, the "nos" are designed to keep them from harm. Too often, though, the "nos" are delivered because of convenience. It is easier for us to discourage children from trying new things because encouragement often requires an investment of time on our own part.

2. In most instances, what keeps people from fulfilling their potential is circumstances beyond their control.
False. As we learned in the previous chapter, most barriers to fulfilling our potential are actually within our control. We can group the perceived barriers into two categories: *internal* and *external*. Internal barriers include fear, lack of confidence, feelings of inferiority, and so on. Although it takes time, persistence, and patience, we can directly control our internal barriers. That's good news because it means we don't have to (and shouldn't) rely on others to overcome them for us.

What about external barriers? Most people believe that they are beyond our control: "Management keeps changing the plan," "My budget has been reduced," "We're in the midst of a merger," "We're downsizing." It's very easy to adopt the victim mentality. A person with a victim mentality is always looking for excuses to explain away his or her performance problems. Yes, it is true that we are often not consulted when decisions are made and that many of us do suffer from the consequences of other people's decisions and actions. It may be true that external events are beyond our direct control, but we can change our *view* of those events.

A manager from a large technology company told me recently that his business unit had run into some problems because of a particular executive. The executive's style was extremely demanding, intolerant, and impatient. His direct reports had begun grumbling about the situation to one another, sending countless e-mails back and forth to blow off steam. The manager received an average of thirty-five negative e-mails about the situation *per day*. Of course, everyone felt compelled to read them all and respond with his or her own particular gripes. This had had an enormous impact on productivity. In frustration and despair, the manager asked me for advice on how to deal with the situation. As I probed, it soon became clear that much of the manager's frustration was the result of trying too hard to change the executive. His feelings of despair were due to his realization that he wasn't going to "change the spots on the leopard." We discussed a number of different options on how to deal with the executive. It was determined that a simple shift in how the manager thought about the situation might solve the dilemma. In other words, instead of trying to change the other person, he could change how he viewed the situation. The manager decided to change his style of dealing with the executive. He endeavored to be more thorough when presenting information to him. He took along data to back his ideas and suggestions.

At some point, to the manager's complete surprise, the executive started treating him differently. He seemed more patient and willing to try new ideas. The executive's change in demeanor was also noticed by others in the group. Before long, the counterproductive e-mails all but disappeared. What happened is that by changing his *own* response to the executive, the manager was able to bring about, indirectly, a change in the executive. The point is that everything that happens to us is controllable—either directly or indirectly.

3. Self-confidence is something that can be faked.

True. This one always causes debate. And the response is often one of skepticism: "How can you fake something like self-confidence?" "If you're faking it, then it can't be self-confidence!" There's a certain truth to those arguments, but self-confidence really can be faked, at least for a little while. One of people's greatest fears is public speaking. Our hearts race, our palms sweat, our knees tremble. I'll never forget the time I was asked to deliver a presentation to a large group of quality managers shortly after I joined the quality management consulting firm the Juran Institute. I was extremely nervous, especially since I was fairly young and still "wet behind the ears." I did not feel confident getting up in front of seasoned professionals. I made negative comments to myself such as "Why would they want to listen to me?" "They have much more experience than I." "What can I tell them that they don't already know?" I decided to seek the advice of

Bob, one of my colleagues. He had many years of experience in the industry, as well as in public speaking.

"Scott, my boy," he said, "we all get butterflies before and during presentations. After all these years, I still get them. The trick, though, is to get the butterflies all flying in the same direction." In other words, we all have times when we don't feel confident. And even though we may not be able to eliminate those feelings (butterflies), we can put them aside and move forward. Some people use the expression "Fake it till you make it" as a way of describing this concept. It's important, though, to make a few additional points: As I stated earlier, you can't "fake" anything forever—nor should you try. I am not suggesting that you become insincere or phony. This technique, known as "acting as if," has roots in behavioral psychology. I will discuss it in much greater detail in a later chapter.

4. Saying that someone is a positive thinker is the same as saying that he or she is a Pollyanna.
False. In Pollyanna's defense, she has taken an undeserved "bad rap." Unfortunately, over the years, the expression "Pollyanna" has taken on a negative connotation. The interesting thing is that when queried, most people are not familiar with the origin of the expression. In fact, until recently I was one of those people. A few months ago I conducted a workshop on positive thinking for a well-known beverage company and the Pollyanna issue came up. Some of the participants were unfamiliar with the term "Pollyanna" and asked me to explain. At that point I was unaware of its origins. All I knew was that it was a negative expression. And that's what I told them.

The next morning I received a call from one of the participants: "Hey, Scott, I just wanted to let you know that the expression 'Pollyanna' came from the story by the same name, published in 1913 by Eleanor H. Porter. You should read it because the main character in the story, Pollyanna, was anything but a 'Pollyanna.' " So I found an old, dusty copy in the library and read it. What I discovered is that the original character, Pollyanna, really was a positive thinker. She was orphaned at eleven years of age and forced to live with her mean-spirited Aunt Polly. Pollyanna, whose father was a minister, had learned from his example by always trying to find the good in every situation. Although life had dealt her a difficult hand, she managed to maintain an even disposition and a positive, hope-filled outlook on life. As a result, she was able to bring about incredible changes in the most negative people—particularly her aunt. So, to clarify the response to question 4, the original character Pollyanna really *was* a positive thinker. But based on our misplaced perceptions, Pollyanna was a naïve, unrealistic child. The distinguishing characteristic of positive thinkers is that they make the best of challenging situations. They are reality-based and tackle problems head-on. A more detailed description of positive thinking comes at the end of this chapter.

5. Our beliefs shape our behavior, which in turn shapes our feelings.
False. At first glance, the order of this statement looks logical. In fact, it is slightly out of order. We often confuse feelings and emotions with behaviors. The correct order is that our beliefs, which are responsible for our thoughts, shape our *feelings*, which in turn shape our *behavior*. Feelings and behaviors are often confused in what appears to be a "chicken-and-egg" dilemma. Which comes first, the feeling or the behavior? I'll explore this concept in more depth in the next chapter.

6. Sometimes you have to ignore facts to be a positive thinker.
True (with clarification). This one always creates animated debate when discussed in groups. "What do you mean, you have to ignore the facts?" bellowed an irate financial analyst attending a positive thinking workshop. "If I ignored facts, I'd be out of a job in no time flat!" "If being a positive thinker means that you don't pay attention to facts, then I want nothing to do with it," said another. The word that evokes such strong reactions is "ignore." This is not to suggest that we should not be aware of and acknowledge facts. It simply means that before we abandon an idea or course of action because of a certain set of facts, we should consider suspending or temporarily ignoring the facts to allow us to remain open to new sets of facts. For instance, I'm a huge Starbucks fan. In his book *Pour Your Heart into It*, Starbucks Chairman and CEO Howard Schultz talks about all the naysayers he had met up with when trying to grow his coffee business. There were plenty of reasons, based on facts, not to proceed with his ideas, he

writes: "We had no lock on the world's supply of fine coffee, no patent on the dark roast. . . . I heard all the arguments about why coffee could never be a growth industry. It was the second most widely traded commodity in the world, after oil. Consumption of coffee had been falling in America since the mid-60s." Many people also told him that people would not pay premium prices for premium coffee. Of course, he proved them wrong. Starbucks has thousands of stores throughout the country and opens hundreds more each year.

Howard acted *despite* the facts and the conclusions drawn from those facts. The key is to identify facts, acknowledge them, and then creatively discover ways of moving forward. Too many of us allow facts to bury us. Instead of using them to our advantage, we transform them into barriers and ultimately into excuses for not taking a particular course of action.

Many great ideas are never implemented in companies because of this syndrome. I remember a few years back when a COO of a large manufacturing company was lamenting about the poor performance of one of his operating companies. Overall, the plant was hitting its numbers, but, as the COO put it, "They're too conservative and not pushing the boundaries. They make their numbers each year, but they're too afraid to go much beyond the previous year's performance. They treat new-product development the same way—very conservatively, with only a few new product introductions per year." Upon further probing, it turned out that the management team was basing its projections on the previous year's performance. That approach in itself is not so bad, as it provides a basis on which to make projections. The problem was that the management team was allowing the "facts" to shackle its thinking. According to the COO, they collectively believed that it was impossible to achieve much beyond 15 percent annual growth and that they could launch only two or three new products in a given year—because they'd never done otherwise. The key to dealing with known facts is that sometimes we have to *seek other facts*. That is, we need to acknowledge the existing facts but also look for new or overlooked facts.

Another example is the story of Roger Bannister. He was the first human being in recorded history to run a sub-four-minute mile. Up until 1954, no one had been able to achieve that feat. The "experts" at the time (physiologists, medical doctors, and others) argued that it was humanly impossible to run a mile in less than four minutes. They presented facts that "proved" that the human body simply was not designed for it. Bannister was not convinced, though. And in 1954 he became the first human being to break the four-minute mark. There's an interesting phenomenon attached to this story; during the next eighteen months, twenty-four more people broke the four-minute mark! Incredible! What happened? Did they try some new steroid or vitamin or sneaker? Did they train harder? No, none of the above. What happened is that they began to believe that it was possible because Bannister had introduced a new set of "facts." Remember, Bannister was aware of the facts before he attempted to run a four-minute mile. And although "ignore" is a strong word, he consciously decided to push the facts aside.

7. We cannot change the reality of most situations; we can control only our responses to it.
True. All too often we get caught up in trying to change things that are beyond our control. That's a waste of both time and energy. We cannot go back and undo the events of the past, and we generally do not have direct influence over the decisions and actions of others. As a result, most of the things that happen to us are beyond our control, and we don't like that. We prefer being in control. But as discussed earlier in this chapter, we have complete control over our *responses* to situations.

8. Our self-expectations are usually not predictors of achievement.
False. In fact, quite the opposite is true: self-expectations are very much a predictor of future success or failure. As Dr. Peale put it, "Expect the best and get the best, expect the worst and get the worst." Like a magnet, positive expectations draw the best to us, while negative expectations draw the worst to us. When we expect success, we change our inner selves fundamentally. Our attitude becomes hopeful and confident. This positive disposition is conveyed in our body language and our written and verbal expression. This in turn affects the people around us in positive ways.

Have you ever met a salesperson you just couldn't say no to? I remember years ago, when I was working as a shipping and receiving manager, I got a call from our receptionist, Maria: "Scott, I have a gentleman here in the main lobby wanting to speak to you. He said he doesn't have an appointment, but would you mind talking to him for just a minute?" I wavered but she persisted, so I met with him (I still remember his name: James), and eventually he earned my business. She told me later that he had made such a positive impression on her that she simply couldn't turn him away. He had been cheerful and persistent without being pushy or rude. Several months later I asked James, "How did you ever persuade our receptionist to call me out to see you that day you came to see me without an appointment?" He told me that he always approached situations with a hopeful, expectant frame of mind. That attitude drove certain positive behaviors, which in turn made a positive impression on Maria, which is why she had responded positively.

9. Facts are more important than attitude.
False. As discussed, our view of the facts is much more important than the facts themselves. In essence, if you think you can overcome an obstacle, chances are you can.

10. If you don't make choices in your life, others will make them for you.
True. Life is full of choices. When we fail to make our own decisions, we often put ourselves at the mercy of others. Positive thinking enables us to make decisions because it removes the causes of indecisiveness: fear, worry, confusion, and other negative emotions.

The modern concepts of positive thinking originated with Dr. Norman Vincent Peale. When I joined his organization, the Peale Center for Christian Living, to develop a workshop for businesses based on his best-selling book *The Power of Positive Thinking*, the first thing I did was go through his private library. It was important to me to develop a program based on a complete understanding of what had shaped his thinking and his views on positive thinking. I was floored by the number and types of books he had read. The more I studied him, the more I realized how much truth and power were behind positive thinking. Based on a number of biographies I read, as well as discussions with his family, I discovered that there had been a number of influences in his life that had shaped his message:

- **His upbringing.** His father was a Methodist minister, and his mother had a great practical faith. They, among other great influences in his early childhood, served as great exemplars of positive thinking.
- **His religion.** As a Methodist, he subscribed to the Puritan ethic, which, in part, tells us to "pull ourselves up by our bootstraps," work hard, and live cleanly.
- **His own personal characteristics.** As a boy he was small and skinny, with a tremendous inferiority complex. He wanted desperately to be bigger, more robust, and more self-confident but was often discouraged because, try as he might, he couldn't seem to change. As he struggled, he found hope through a number of experiences.

One was when, as a young schoolboy, his teacher wrote the word "can't" on the blackboard—and, to make the point how easy it was to go from a negative "can't" to a positive "can," took an eraser and swiped the " 't" right off the board. The metaphor remained with him his whole life.

- **The period in which he lived.** Dr. Peale lived through arguably the most negative period of our history: the Great Depression and World Wars I and II. People were despondent, discouraged, ravaged by war, and grief-stricken at the loss of their loved ones. He saw firsthand how positive thinking could turn negative situations around.
- **His keen interest in psychology.** He was particularly fond of the writings of Dr. William James, a professor at Harvard, who is known as the "father of modern psychology."
- **His keen interest in the great poets and philosophers.** These included Ralph Waldo Emerson, Ralph Waldo Trine, Marcus Aurelius, and more.

Consequently, his concept of positive thinking was a blend of all of these influences but was based primarily on spirituality and psychology. For Peale, the term "positive thinking" was synonymous with faith. He believed that with faith in God, all things are possible. Faith in God, he believed, drives belief in self, leading to self-confidence. Psychology plays an important role because it is primarily through the mind that we experience God and communicate with him, he thought. This is one of the reasons, I believe, why Dr. Peale did not drink alcohol. It would have impaired his ability to experience and communicate with God, the source of positive thinking.

A DESCRIPTION OF POSITIVE THINKING

Now that you have some background and history on what shaped the message of positive thinking, let us look at an expanded definition. Positive thinking:

- Is our innate capability to produce desired outcomes with positive thoughts.
- Is having a belief in possibilities even when the facts seem to indicate otherwise.
- Is a composite of ten traits.
- Involves making creative choices.
- Meets problems head-on.

Remember,

- Positive and negative thoughts both contain facts.
- Negative thinking is mostly learned.
- Hence, we can unlearn negative thinking and rediscover positive thinking.

Now that we have been over the basics of positive thinking, let's explore the first major step in how to make it happen in the workplace.

Part Two

FROM DESTRUCTIVE THOUGHTS TO POSITIVE GOALS

3

How the Mind Works

*Pat, who holds a midlevel administrative job, is always bubbling with
new ideas. Unfortunately, most of them are daydreams and have no
practical value. This does not faze Pat. When an idea occurs to her,
she wants to share it immediately, and usually with her team leader,
Jan. Now Pat has come up with another idea and has dropped by Jan's
office to speak to her. "Jan, this will only take a minute, but I've got an
incredible idea I want to tell you about, and this time I think I'm
really onto something big!" she says with her usual enthusiasm.
Meanwhile, as Pat proceeds, Jan begins shuffling through some
papers, looking through her mail, and fidgeting with some paper clips.
Undaunted, Pat continues, "This idea will allow us to break into a
new market that promises to yield high margins . . ." At this point the
phone rings, and Jan picks it up and starts talking about the stock
market and other nonrelated issues. Noticing Jan's lack of attention,
Pat abruptly stops talking and storms out of the office.*

Pat is obviously upset about Jan's inattention. How would *you* have
reacted if you were Pat? Would you have had the same reaction?
Would your reaction have been different? How?

All of our reactions to situations manifest themselves *behaviorally.*
And because we are unique individuals, our reactions or behaviors
vary from person to person and situation to situation. But no matter
how different we are, our behaviors are the result of our thoughts,
both conscious and subconscious. One of Dr. William James's most

important discoveries was that we *think,* then *feel* something as a result of the thought, then *act* based on the feeling. As Emerson so aptly put it, "The thought is the predecessor to the deed." When you understand this concept of thought, feeling, and action, you can begin to gain control over your negative feelings (emotions) and actions (behaviors) by changing the negative thoughts, from which the negative feelings and actions emanate, to positive ones.

The T-F-A Chain

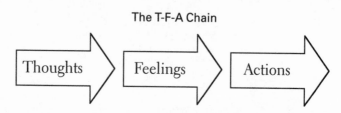

Let's get back to Pat. If we apply the thoughts-feelings-actions (T-F-A) chain to Pat, what do you think it would look like? Pat's action was storming out of the office. What feeling or feelings do you suppose led her to react in such a way? Although we can only guess, one might say that she felt angry, hurt, disappointed, and frustrated. What were the thoughts that led to such emotions? Again we can only speculate, but she might have been telling herself some of the following things:

"Jan never takes me seriously. What she did was rude and inconsiderate."
"I've spend days working through these ideas, and the least she can do is look at me when I'm talking."
"Once again I've failed to communicate a new idea effectively. Will I ever get it right?"

Each of these thoughts is likely to produce negative feelings. Each negative feeling leads to negative actions. Negative actions lead to negative consequences. It's the consequences of negative actions that cause so much trouble in the workplace. And as discussed in the first chapter, that's why negative thinking costs companies so much money.

Pat does have a choice: she can change her thoughts about the treatment she is receiving from Jan. Keep in mind that nearly all situations at work, no matter how frustrating or challenging, have a positive side. If you focus on the positive, you will be in a far better position, both mentally and emotionally, to respond to a given situation in a thoughtful, logical, constructive manner. The truth is that most of us have been in a position like Pat's. Was Pat's response justified, or could she have behaved in a more positive, constructive way? Using the T-F-A model, Pat could have orchestrated a more positive outcome by changing her *thoughts* about her conversation with Jan to more positive ones. For instance, she might have told herself any of the following things:

"I probably caught Jan by surprise. Next time I'll schedule an appointment."

"I'm sure Jan has a lot on her mind; maybe I should write my ideas out on paper and have her review them before we discuss them."

"Although I don't like not being paid attention to, I do have a creative mind and tend to bombard people with lots of new ideas. Jan may perceive this as yet one more far-out idea. I need to be more patient with her."

What kinds of *feelings* would these particular thoughts have evoked? They'd very likely have been more positive. She'd have felt more calm and patient. Feelings of calm and patience transform themselves into positive *actions*. As a result, Pat might have simply excused herself, requesting to meet at a more appropriate time. No matter how unfairly we think we have been treated, we should always give the other person the benefit of the doubt; we never know what might be going on in her life that might cause her to act in such a way.

We are always interpreting other people's behaviors. And most of the time, our interpretations are either wrong or inaccurate. It is tempting to fall into this trap because we cannot read people's thoughts, but our false or harsh judgments feed our negative "self-talk." It's OK, though to describe the behavior you are observing to the other person, as long as you do not interpret it. For instance, Pat might have said, "Jan, it looks as though you're extremely busy. Is there a better time when we can meet?" I'm not suggesting that we excuse people for being inconsiderate or rude. I do believe, though, that it's always better to take the high road in our dealings with them. We never know what's going on in other people's minds until, as the Native American saying goes, "we've walked a mile in their moccasins."

Sometimes we have to deal with certain people in influential positions who, for whatever reason, make our lives miserable. We question how they ever got to be in a position of authority in the first place. No matter where we go, we will experience people like this, making positive self-talk virtually impossible. At times like that, sometimes the best we can do is accept that we cannot directly change other people. We need to make a conscious decision to let go. Worrying or being negative about things we cannot change will improve neither them nor your life.

Changing our thoughts from negative to positive ones requires that we take a close look at our self-talk. Self-talk is like having a CD player in your head; it's burned into the mind. When faced with various situations, we automatically hit the "play" button. Your boss is not listening to you, so you go to disc 2, track 8: "The boss is a jerk." Or management is restructuring again, so you go to disc 4, track 1: "Those morons have no idea what they're doing."

By listening to our self-talk, we can discover whether or not our responses, especially to tough, challenging situations, are rational and constructive or irrational and destructive. How you talk to yourself all day long has a major impact on how you feel and perform. Think of something that is going on right now at work and that happens to be particularly challenging. What "tracks" do you hear being played in your mind? Whatever you say to yourself is an example of self-talk. The fact is, we all talk to ourselves all day long. If you are thinking, you are talking to yourself and seeing flashes of images as well.

The implications of this simple fact are profound when you consider the fact that your present thoughts (in the form of self-talk) determine your feelings, which determine your actions. Simply put, if you want to feel good and be as effective and efficient as possible, talk to yourself in a positive manner. This requires seeing the positive side of situations and people, not just the negative. Here are some examples of self-sabotaging, negative self-talk:

"As usual, the situation is normal—all fouled up."
"I can't catch a break."
"This is killing me. I can't take it anymore."
"This is do or die. I'm going to choke."
"Here goes nothing."
"I'm not a writer. Why do I have to prepare this report?"
"He's a louse. I can't stand him."
"Oh yeah, like they really care about us."
"They've never bought from us before; I don't know why they should now."
"Every time I call them, I get the runaround."
"If this works, it will be a miracle."
"I'm no good at this."
"I'm such a jerk. How could I make a mistake like that?"

"When the mind talks, the body listens. We literally talk ourselves into and out of every victory or defeat in the game of life." So says Dr. Denis Waitley, a scientist who has studied human performance for more than twenty years.

Professional and Olympic athletes, for example, say things such as "I'm getting a base hit this time," "Need a ten, got a ten," "I'm unstoppable." Earlier I talked about the "three Ls": Lack, Loss, and Limitation. Self-talk that centers on lacking a resource, such as time, money, or information; that dwells on a past loss or the possibility of a future one ("Here we go again, the same lousy outcome as last time I tried this"); or that focuses on a personal limitation ("I don't have the proper background and experience") while ignoring personal strengths is very likely to set one up for failure. *What the mind dwells upon, the body acts upon.*

As you go through the day, monitor your self-talk. Whenever you catch yourself saying something negative about yourself, other people, or the situation you are in, see if you can find a positive characteristic to focus on. Both viewpoints are true and equally valid, but one helps you to think creatively and get what you want while the other limits your options, thereby working against you.

THE SITUATION TRANSFORMATION TECHNIQUE

Viewing challenging, adverse situations positively takes practice. And with practice, we can condition our automatic responses to emerge in a positive manner. Suppose you have just learned that as a result of downsizing, you'll be losing your job in a month. Your negative self-talk might be:

"I'm too old. I'll never find another job."
"How will I ever pay my bills?"
"Why me? They should have let John go instead."

This kind of talk can lead us to make rash, hasty decisions. As a result, we might take the first job that comes along, put our home up for sale, or become depressed or physically ill from worry.

Transforming these negative thoughts into positive ones requires that we identify all the potential benefits of a situation. Here are a few possible examples of positive self-talk pertaining to the downsizing situation:

"I'm actually relieved, I've been in a rut anyhow. This is the kick in the pants I needed."
"I'm a smart, energetic, and dedicated person. I'll find work, no problem. It'll take a little time, but I'm resourceful."
"This will give me an opportunity to spend time with my family while I explore new career paths."

How we choose to view the situation makes all the difference in the world. American semanticist and U.S. senator S. I. Hayakawa once said, "Notice the difference between what happens when a man says to himself, 'I have failed three times,' and what happens when he says, 'I am a failure.'" The latter statement personalizes the "failure." Feelings of worthlessness and self-pity arise from such negative self-talk. The former suggests that although certain goals were not achieved, there will be more opportunities.

Changing our self-talk to be more positive yields dramatic results. No matter how pessimistic or negative you may think you are, we are all endowed with the ability to view things more positively. Some people seem to have a knack for maintaining a steady, even, calm disposition in trying times, while others get upset over every little thing.

WHY DO PEOPLE RESPOND SO DIFFERENTLY TO THE SAME SITUATIONS?

It's Monday morning. There's a pall over the office. Instead of engaging in the usual "How was your weekend?" chitchat, employees are gathered in small groups in serious discussion. What's up?

It doesn't take long to learn that the department manager was summoned to a special meeting that lasted all day Sunday; the meeting resumed early this morning and is still going on.

Rumors range from a corporate takeover to a major downsizing to a total reorganization of the company.

Productivity is at a standstill. Suddenly the manager comes in. She looks grave. All eyes are on her. She looks around and says, "We'll meet in the conference room in one hour."

Everyone is obviously concerned. They're uncertain about what's going on and how they will be affected. What's everybody thinking? What are they telling themselves? Getting to the *source* of our negative self-talk is the key to ridding ourselves of it forever.

4

Getting to the Source of Negative Thoughts

Many factors contribute to how we view circumstances in our lives and react to them. Ultimately, our views and reactions are based on our *beliefs* about how the world should work. When we add "beliefs" to the T-F-A chain, discussed in the previous chapter, it becomes clear that our actions result from our feelings, which result from our thoughts, which result from our beliefs. It follows, then, that the key to changing negative actions is to identify and eliminate—or reduce greatly—our self-limiting beliefs.

Some people see struggle and challenge as natural, unavoidable parts of life. Others hold the belief that life should not or must not be so tough. But we can't change the reality of situations, only our responses to them. The psychologist who pioneered cognitive psychology, Dr. Albert Ellis, discovered that beliefs (how one views the world and life in general) are the sources of one's thoughts. If one's beliefs are predominately rational, that is, compatible with the realities of life, one's thoughts will be generally realistic and constructive, leading to constructive feelings and actions. If one's beliefs are irrational or self-limiting, incompatible with the realities of life, one's thoughts will be, for the most part, unrealistic and self-limiting, leading to negative feelings and ineffective actions. *The fact that our thoughts emanate from our individual beliefs about the world and life in general provides us with tremendous insight into how we can change negative actions into positive actions.*

The B-F-T-A Chain

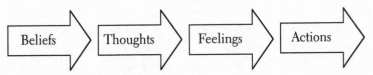

SELF-LIMITING BELIEFS

So where do we start? Almost all negative thoughts, feelings, and actions can be attributed to self-limiting beliefs. The following is a list of universally held self-limiting beliefs.

1. People must treat me fairly.
2. I should have little discomfort in life.
3. People must find me likable.
4. It's awful when I make a mistake.
5. I must perform well or I'm no good.
6. People who treat me badly deserve to be punished.
7. I must get what I want when I want it.
8. I cannot control how I feel.

Let's take a closer look at each one of these universal self-limiting beliefs (SLBs), including some phrases associated with each, and show how they affect workplace performance.

1. People must treat me fairly.

"How can they do that to me after all I've done for them?"

"My team just doesn't appreciate all the help I've given them!"

"After twenty years of loyal, dedicated service, I'm downsized out of here."

"I worked so hard on my presentation, how dare they not like it?"

"But Carol has a new computer, why can't I have one?"

What happens if we hold this SLB and someone does not treat us fairly? We are likely to be disappointed and perhaps vindictive. Many people have the philosophy "If I treat others fairly, they had better treat me in kind." There's nothing wrong with expecting fair treatment in exchange for giving it. Some people even expect fair treatment regardless of how they treat others. Sometimes it's our perceptions and definition of the word "fairness" that cause the self-limiting belief. A few weeks ago I was having a discussion with one of my clients. He was upset because he had been passed by for a big promotion.

"Scott," he said, "I've been here for ten years and have worked hard. I've paid my dues. They [management] told me that I was the top candidate for the position. I can't believe they did this to me!"

He was so disappointed that although he liked his job and the company, he was considering leaving. He felt that because he had seniority and knew the job inside and out, he should have been rewarded with the promotion. It seemed like a logical conclusion. As I continued to probe, however, some additional information emerged that helped explain management's decision.

I asked him about his relationships with his boss, peers, and direct reports. He shared an incident that had occurred a few years before. Apparently he'd had a run-in with someone who had later become a key manager in the organization. Upon reflection, my client admitted that, at the time, he had been new to management and had still not completely mastered people skills. This might have been the reason he hadn't gotten the promotion. So although originally he had felt he was being treated unfairly because he believed he met the requirements for the new position, after considering the situation more carefully, he realized that the other person might not have had the same experience but on balance was the better candidate. I urged him to channel his anger and frustration into constructive activities. For instance, I suggested that he gather more information about himself and the specific areas he could improve upon — and not just to get the next promotion, but to help him grow as a human being. The bottom line is that the world and the people in it are often unfair. We cannot avoid unfairness, but we can learn how to react to it with a more positive frame of mind.

2. I should have little discomfort in life.

"Here we go again, another reorganization. Why do they have to do this to me?"

"I can't believe they want me to go back to training to learn about the new computer system. What a waste of time!"

"Like I really need the aggravation of rewriting the proposal right now!"

"Why can't they get back to me with an answer on the proposal? They're taking forever to make a decision."

"What a hassle to have to write all these reports. They don't read half of them anyway!"

This SLB is very selfish. It hurts organizations because it prevents people from taking risks and trying new opportunities. It is the primary reason why we give up on a project, endeavor, or person—we simply quit when things become unpleasant or painful. A friend of mine is the head of human resources for a small professional services firm. Fore more than a year, he had been complaining about one of the managing partners. The partner had a nasty temper and would frequently blow up at people with little provocation. My friend was at a loss as to how to deal with this individual. He had been overlooking the disruptive behavior because it would have been too uncomfortable and unpleasant to deal with it. As time went on, things got worse, causing a great deal of upheaval and turmoil. He decided to deal with the situation directly, firmly, and courageously by confronting the partner. He aired all his concerns, aggravations, and frustrations. The partner did not take it well and reacted in a hostile manner, as my friend had predicted. But once the confrontation was over, the problem was solved, and as a result the business (as well as my friend) became much stronger.

One manager who attended my positive thinking workshop told me that he had been having performance problems with a certain employee whom he had "inherited" from another department. He said that instead of addressing performance issues, the other managers would recommend problem employees for promotion *in another department*. They simply didn't want all the annoyance that confronting the employees would entail. It was far easier to move the "problems" to some other place. No one likes pain and discomfort. We go out of our way to avoid them, but when we do everyone loses as a result; an employee loses an opportunity to learn and grow, a new manager inherits a performance problem, and the organization is less productive. People who have accomplished great things have done so by sacrificing and suffering greatly. In my professional life, my times of greatest growth have occurred during the times when I felt the most despair and discouragement. Unfortunately, many of us either never try to work through problems or quit just shy of the goal line because things get too rough. The amount of gain is proportionate to the amount of pain we experience: "No pain, no gain."

3. People must find me likable.

"What did I do to cause Sue to dislike me so much?"

"I'm going to compliment Keith on his cost-saving plan, even though I don't think it's all that great."

"Nobody likes me. That's why I never get any good opportunities around here."

"I couldn't stand it if Bob was mad at me!"

Many wrong decisions are made and wrong actions taken in business because we fear being rejected or disapproved of by other people. For some of us, the need to be accepted and to fit in is so strong that we fail to be honest with other people about their actions. "If I tell Keith what I *really* think of his idea, he'd be upset with me for a long time. I have to work with him every day—I couldn't handle it." It is okay to want to be liked by others; in fact, according to psychologist Abraham Maslow, it is one of people's strongest needs. But insisting that people "must" find you likable influences your conduct negatively. An accounting manager told me that although she never knew exactly *why* she did it, she would often adjust her ratings and comments during performance appraisal time for certain people—she did not want to offend people and risk their not liking her.

A better, more constructive way of dealing with our need to be liked is to focus on our self-respect. We *can't* make people like us; what we *can* do is work on ourselves. We can think, feel, and act more securely and confidently; people are attracted to these traits. We can also concentrate on liking others versus being liked by others. So instead of being absorbed by our own needs, we can think more about the needs of others in a sincere way, without any expectation of personal gain. I remember talking to my cousin Phil about this subject one afternoon. As always, he had a very interesting perspective (and solution) that has stuck with me to this day. He said, "You know, Scott, people try to win the approval of others by trying to be *interesting*. They talk about themselves most of the time. They never ask questions of the other person, and when the other person speaks they don't listen. Instead of trying to be interest*ing*, we should try harder to be interest*ed* in the other person." If we are genuinely interested in other people, they will respond positively.

4. It's awful when I make a mistake.
"I'm no good, I can't get anything right!"
"What an idiot, I can't believe I just did that."
"I don't deserve a second chance."
"I'll never get the promotion now."
"It's way too risky, I'd better not try it."
"I just can't make a decision because it might be the wrong one."

The feeling of worthlessness that comes over us when we make a mistake is often caused by our recollections of how others have reacted to our mistakes over the course of our lives. Perhaps a former boss, a teacher, or a parent berated us about them.

Many people don't even know why they feel worthless—or care, for that matter. Carrying this self-limiting belief into the workplace, though, has many negative consequences. I once worked with a fast-food chain headquartered in the Northeast to help it determine the causes of the low customer satisfaction in one of its regional outlets. A cross-functional team was formed that included the store manager, a cook, and a cashier. We had discovered some of the causes of the low customer satisfaction and were preparing to brainstorm potential remedies. As the facilitator, I noticed that during the brainstorming process, one of the team members kept "passing" when it was her turn. Not wanting to embarrass her in front of the others, I approached her afterward to ask why she had kept passing on her turn. She told me that she had been afraid she'd be wrong or have a stupid idea and the others would laugh at her. She was a young single mother without a high school degree and felt worthless. I reminded

her that she was considered a hardworking, dedicated, and resourceful employee, which was why management had decided to train her
and put her on the team. I encouraged her to participate in the next
brainstorming session, which she did. As it turned out, one of her
ideas in particular was the key to solving the problem. Companies are
filled with people who are afraid to try anything new—an idea, position, or technology—because they don't want to make a mistake. An
essential managerial attribute is having the ability to make decisions,
but many decisions are never made because of managers' desire to
avoid making mistakes.

5. I must perform well or I'm no good.

"If I don't get the top job, forget it, I'm a failure."
"I can't believe I missed the deadline. My manager must think I'm
  a total jerk."
"Things had better go smoothly, because if they don't I'll look re-
  ally bad."
"I better not make a move just yet—I may not have all the infor-
  mation."
"They have to pick my idea, or I'm a miserable failure."

This is very similar to the previous SLB, but it can cause even more
damage. As a consultant I have had the opportunity to work with many
good companies and have met some extremely bright people over the
years. It is amazing how many people I've met whose happiness depends upon how well they perform, who feel that anything less than
perfection is failure. What I find so interesting is that this feeling is *self-
imposed*. Unlike the previous SLB, its source is what I believe is an inherent competitiveness. I've met many managers who have admitted
that their fiercest competitor was themselves! In fact, they're harder on
themselves than they are on their employees.

As an adjunct business school professor, I have had many talented
students who have been incredibly hard on themselves. I remember
receiving a call from a very bright student asking what he could do to
bring his grade up from an A minus to an A: "I just gotta have an A,
Professor, if I don't my GPA will drop below 4.0! I couldn't live with

myself if that happened." Some students abuse themselves mentally and physically if they fall short of their goals. We live in an achievement-oriented society, and regardless of the causes, some of us view ourselves as failures if we don't measure up 100 percent all the time. This has a dual effect on workplace performance, too: (1) A perfectionist takes much more time and resources to complete certain tasks than is necessary; the benefits of seeking perfection are not commensurate with the extra effort required to reach it. (2) As we are fallible human beings, our idea of perfection, when not attained, often leads to depression and anxiety.

6. People who treat me badly deserve to be punished.

"It's your fault that this is happening."
"John will pay for that if it's the last thing I do."
"She's finally going to get what's coming to her."
"That's the last time I do anything for Mary."

It's difficult to calculate the costs associated with "getting even" with people who have done us wrong. Few people would admit that they spend time and energy on doing so. In a previous SLB, "People must treat me fairly," we learned that we all have an idea of how we should be treated. This particular SLB is one of the consequences of feeling that we are not being treated fairly. We name ourselves judge and jury and devise a punishment to fit the crime. This has a negative impact on an organization because it converts positive energy, which could be used in productive ways, into negative energy.

Punishment is dealt out in a number of ways: undermining another's efforts, criticizing the "offender's" ideas, gossip intending to hurt or destroy, and so on. A report in *The Wall Street Journal* cited a survey conducted by the University of North Carolina Business School that noted that as a result of incivility 22 percent of the respondents indicated that they had deliberately decreased their output and 52 percent said that they had lost time at work worrying. In its most severe form, punishment is aimed at the company by an employee who feels that he or she has been wronged. A few years back, a well-known NFL player admitted that while working on an automobile assembly line, he had placed loose hardware (nuts, bolts, and washers) inside the door frame that would rattle like crazy when the car was driven. He felt that he had been wronged by the automaker and "was getting back at them."

A healthier mind-set in dealing with injustice and incivility is to realize that most of the people we deal with are basically good people. But even basically good people can do "bad" things—and most of the time they are unintentional. There's a great line toward the end of the classic movie *The Wizard of Oz*. Dorothy, feeling cheated by the wizard, chastises him, saying, "You're a very bad man!" His reply is "Oh no, my dear, I'm just a bad wizard!"—although some of his actions in his role as wizard are bad, he is basically a good man.

We don't need to obsess about getting even with people. The energy we expend on the job can be put to either positive use or negative use. I am convinced that we should never use negative energy to deal with negative situations. If anything, we should either redirect the energy in more useful ways or meet the negative energy with positive energy. Negative energy crumbles under the enormous power of positive energy. Overcoming negative energy takes time, resolve, and fortitude, but eventually one will prevail. In the course of my professional life, I have negotiated many deals and contracts. In one case, a dispute arose regarding the interpretation of certain language in the contract. I felt I was being treated unfairly. My first reaction was to hire a lawyer and go after the offending party. After I thought about it, though, I realized I would spend far too much time and energy on something that in the grand scheme of things was not that important to me. I let it go and redirected my efforts into growing my business. The sweet feelings of revenge are brief, leaving a bitter aftertaste as we reflect on our return on investment. As tempting as revenge may be and as justified as you may feel, stay away from vindictiveness—it only creates more negative energy.

7. I must get what I want when I want it.

"Come on, let's go, I don't have all day!"

"If you don't have the analysis completed by tomorrow, you can just forget it!"

"Never mind what Smith wants, I need you on this assignment now."

"You'll have to reprioritize, this is too important to me."

When I see this SLB, I'm reminded of a song from a Broadway musical. Although I don't remember the name of the musical, I do remember some of the lyrics, which go like this: "I want what I want when I want it, and I want it *now!*" This SLB is based on a feeling of self-importance. It drives impatient, demanding behavior, throwing an organization into turmoil. Self-importance and the feeling that the world revolves around oneself come from various sources. People growing up in environments where everything was handed to them on a silver platter, or who have attained a certain status in life, often adopt this attitude. If we don't learn how to deal with it, we risk driving good people away. How many times have you heard this from a friend or coworker: "No matter how hard I try, I just can't seem to please him." When I started my consulting career, my first big assignment was with a well-known educational service organization. It was one of the most difficult assignments I have ever been involved in. The organization had an overwhelmingly large number of Ph.D.s, and although that in and of itself is not a bad thing, several of them made life miserable for others because they were so demanding. Having worked in that environment, I made the observation that those without advanced degrees seemed to bear the brunt of the unreasonable demands the most.

Individuals with this attitude are not likely to change overnight. Changing it requires a greater understanding and tolerance of others. We have to remind ourselves that we're not the center of the universe. Other people have other goals and priorities that don't always fit into our scheme of things.

8. I cannot control how I feel.

"That's just the way I am, there's nothing I can do about it."

"Look, I've always been like this, you'll have to get used to it."

"Who wouldn't react this way?"

"I'm sorry I hollered at you, I can't help it."

I call this SLB "the big excuse." It covers for a lot of inappropriate behavior: yelling, ranting and raving, name-calling, and other unprofessional conduct. I know of people who have been plagued with this problem, and it has hurt them professionally. It has derailed many promising careers. I remember talking to someone who was upset with himself because he often lost control of his temper. He realized that if he did so one more time, he'd be fired, as he had been warned on a number of occasions. "I'm afraid this is it for me," he told me. "You see, Scott, I've been like this all my life. I want to change, but I can't. It's just the way I am." This is a sad statement. It's filled with self-defeating language. It suggests that things are unchangeable. And until they are forced, most people with this attitude won't do anything about it. People will often cite their personal history ("It's the way I was brought up"), ethnic background ("I'm Italian, we're all emotional"), or some significant event in life ("I was teased as a child") as a reason why they can't change. Quite often they are helped by the enablers around them: "Oh, don't mind Pete, that's just the way he is. Don't take it personally." If they don't make excuses for themselves, there's sure to be someone who will. The first step in overcoming this SLB is to believe that no matter how ingrained you might think it is, you can change. People do it all the time. You don't want to wait until your job, your health, or an important relationship is at risk.

According to psychologist Albert Ellis, all self-limiting beliefs can be reduced to one of the three core irrationalities:

1. An impulse to self-denigration
2. Intolerance or frustration
3. Blaming and condemning others

High performers in the workplace are in step with reality. They do not blow things out of proportion or read too much into situations. They accept the fact that difficult people and unpleasant situations come with the territory. They also understand that they are not perfect. They put their inevitable mistakes and failures into perspective, learn from them, and move forward in pursuit of their goals. To some degree, we all have self-limiting beliefs that get in the way of stellar performance. Understanding them and their impact on performance is an important first step in dealing with them. But can we overcome them—and, if so, how?

> *To succeed, it is necessary to accept the world*
> *as it is and rise above it.*
> —MICHAEL KORDA, AMERICAN PUBLISHING
> EXECUTIVE AND AUTHOR

TRUTH IN THINKING

No doubt you have heard the terms "truth in lending" and "truth in advertising." The words "truth in" refer to the disclosure of the accurate, pertinent information consumers need to make informed decisions. Similarly, the "truth in thinking" technique discloses the information (rational beliefs) you need if you are to think, feel, and act constructively in situations you find frustrating or challenging.

Answering the following six questions will help you achieve truth in thinking:

1. What is the event that has triggered your being upset?
2. What are you telling yourself about the event? (What's your self-talk?)
3. Is what you are telling yourself in step with the world as it truly is or merely how you wish (or insist) it to be? (Check your self-talk against the list of self-limiting beliefs.)
4. What is a more realistic, rational, and constructive way of viewing the event?
5. How can viewing the event in a more realistic, rational, and constructive way benefit you and any others involved?
6. How can you change your original self-talk to self-talk that reflects your new perspective on the event?

Let's look at an example. We've all experienced waiting at an airport for a long-delayed flight. It's frustrating and annoying. Our self-talk might sound something like this: "Why does this always have to happen to me? I can't believe it. I'll never make the meeting now." As a result, we sit and stew, lashing out at anybody who comes across our path. Is our reaction rational? Which self-limiting beliefs are at work here? Some of us believe that things should always go smoothly and are intolerant when things don't. A better way of viewing this event is to see the positive aspects of the situation. The delay might be due to bad weather or a mechanical failure, in which case the delay is for our own safety. Viewing it in this way saves us undue annoyance and misery. We can change our self-talk to reflect a more positive mind-set: "I'd rather be safe than sorry. I'll just call and let everyone know that I'll be delayed. Joanne can cover for me anyway if they have to start without me. I'm going to sit back, relax, and catch up on my reading. There's nothing I can do about it anyway."

People are often amazed at the power and effectiveness of this simple process. It's powerful because it helps bring subconscious irrational, self-limiting beliefs up to a conscious level. We see only behaviors; we can't see the subconscious beliefs that are responsible for them. Many times we behave in ways that even we can't explain. For instance, if our behavior was an overly complimentary performance review, few people say to themselves, "The reason I gave Beth such a glowing review, even though she didn't deserve it, is because I have a subconscious, self-limiting belief that people must find me likable." But by being aware of our self-limiting beliefs, we are able to draw links to our negative or self-limiting behaviors. Then, by applying truth in thinking in stressful or upsetting situations, we can begin to minimize those behaviors. I've found that most people won't admit, at least in public, that they possess one or more of the self-limiting beliefs. But seasoned managers have told me, privately, how much this concept has helped them.

According to Albert Ellis, most self-limiting beliefs fall into four basic categories: (1) *awfulizing statements*, which overly dramatize a situation; (2) *should, ought, and must statements*, which are based on unrealistic demands and expectations placed on oneself, others, and situations; (3) *statements of evaluation of human worth*, either of oneself or of others, that imply that some people are of greater or lesser value than others; and (4) *need statements*, which indicate that without a certain want or need being fulfilled, one can't possibly survive or be happy. You may find that your SLBs fall into one category more than another.

If you regularly and diligently apply truth in thinking to your tough situations, over time you will develop an awareness of certain recurring self-limiting beliefs. This will help you get your emotions under control *quickly*. It will also improve your relationships. And remember, our success in business depends upon the commitment, loyalty, and support of those around us.

5

Setting Positive Business Goals, Affirmation, and Visualization

SETTING GOALS

Now that we understand steps one and two in the road map to positive thinking, let's consider step three, setting goals for the specific situation we are addressing. What is your desired outcome? When you define in detail what you want to accomplish—that is, specify your goals—you create a target on which you can focus and leverage your time, talents, energy, and activities. It is no surprise that good managers see *goal setting* as a prerequisite of an organization's success. However, goal setting can be taken a step further by rephrasing goals as *affirmations*—positive, personalized statements that act as superchargers for goal attainment. Further, when added to the goal-setting/affirmation mix, the *visualization* technique improves the likelihood of achieving one's goals by an order of magnitude. Let's first address the whys and hows of goal setting.

A well-written goal can guide you both consciously and unconsciously toward its attainment. It can also help you recognize opportunities to facilitate your progress. By defining each of your major goals in writing, you create a clear mission statement that has the authority of a binding contract with yourself. I have taught goal setting for more than fifteen years and have found a particular method to be especially understandable and useful. It's called the "SMART method." Your goals should be:

- Specific
- Measurable
- Action-oriented
- Realistic
- Time-bound

Specific

A goal should be as *specific* as possible. Generally, the level of specificity depends on the amount of accurate information and data one has. Vaguely written goals do little to inspire and motivate us. For instance, one manager I worked with recently set a goal to "improve response time." I asked him, "To whom do you want to improve your response time, and why?" Challenging his thinking further, I asked, "What do you mean by 'improve' and 'response time'? Can you define those terms for me operationally?" His department served only internal customers and had been receiving a number of complaints about not receiving information in a timely manner. After conducting some research and analysis, he determined that the majority of the complaints had to do with delays in receiving data required by the sales staff, which prevented them from serving their external customers promptly.

After spending some time probing the meaning of the terms, the manager up with the following: "I will reduce the amount of time it takes to respond to my internal customers' request for new pricing information." Compare the first statement to the new one. Can you see the difference? A specific goal helps the goal setter know exactly what to focus on and why.

Measurable

There's an expression, "You can't improve what you can't measure." Without measurement, you'll never know to what extent you've improved your situation. Pre- and postmeasurement are critical in that they provide a basis for comparison. Using our previous example, what aspects of the goal are measurable?

The reduction of time lends itself to measurement. Rewritten, the goal might read, "I will reduce the amount of time it takes to respond to my internal customers' request for new pricing-information *by 25%.*"

Action-oriented

If a goal statement is not action-oriented, it will probably never be achieved. You have to *do* something to make it happen. There should be language indicating what is going to be done about the subject of the goal. As an example, "looking into complaints" will do nothing to help a bad situation. Using language such as "reducing" or "eliminating" complaints is proactive and action-oriented.

Realistic

Your goal should be realistic. The definition of "realistic," however, is in the eye of the beholder. We all have different views on what is attainable and what is not. Of course, we can always look at past performance to establish a benchmark. That is, we can ask ourselves, "What have we been able to do in the past?" We can also ask ourselves, "What are we capable of doing?" I remember working with a team assigned a cost reduction project. The team leader said, "They [management] are asking us to reduce costs by eleven percent over the next six months. We've cut all we possibly can; any more is impossible!"

In this case, the team had no choice. But in their minds, 11 percent was unrealistic because they felt they had already gone as far as they could. In management's mind, though, the goal was realistic. Some people set overly conservative goals. They have the mind-set that it's better to underpromise and overdeliver than vice versa. In general, that can be a safe way of setting a goal. But we're not here to talk about setting safe goals. Positive thinkers set goals that seem just a bit beyond their reach. Challenging goals lean toward the unattainable side and require extra doses of confidence, creativity, and ingenuity. Dr. Peale used to encourage people to adopt the 10 percent rule: whatever goal you set, add 10 percent to it. Force yourself to stretch a bit, and get out of your comfort zone. Using the example of "reducing response time by 25%," we have to ask ourselves, is this realistic? Where did the number come from? Many people set arbitrary measurements for their goals. One way of setting a realistic goal is to look at actual performance. What is the current response time? It's important to establish a baseline. Next, what are the benchmarks either inside or outside your organization? If others can respond in X amount of time, there's no reason to believe you can't.

Time-bound

When do you envision achieving your goal? Open-ended goals give us the luxury of taking our time. There's no great urgency compelling us to be diligent about doing so. A goal that is set to be achieved at some point fairly far in the future, for example beyond three months away, should be broken down into stages with predetermined milestones for its completion.

For instance, "reducing costs due to poor quality in FY 2001 by 8%" might be broken down like this: "reduce scrap by X% in the first quarter of FY 2001," "reduce customer returns by Y% in the second quarter of FY 2001," and so on. All Olympic competitors set goals for themselves and then break them down into bite-sized pieces. Breaking down each major goal into pieces makes accomplishing them more focused, less intimidating, and more easily scheduled into one's daily and weekly routine. Here are three pairs of sample goal statements. Review each one using the SMART criteria. Which statement in each pair does a better job of meeting the criteria?

1a. "I need to hire more people this year."
1b. "This quarter, I will hire three marketing representatives with e-commerce experience."

2a. "This month, I will meet with my top three customers to determine their product and service needs for the coming year."
2b. "This month, I will meet socially with my top three customers to strengthen our business relationships."

3a. "This quarter, I will empower my staff to reduce my workload, enabling me to take on more strategic projects."
3b. "By the end of this quarter, I will identify three tasks that regularly take up my time and delegate them to Jim and Barbara, enabling me to take on more strategic projects."

If you chose 1b, 2a, and 3b, you are correct. Each includes additional information that comes closer to meeting the SMART criteria than the other in the pair.

AFFIRMATION

Once you have set your goals using the SMART criteria, change your statement into an affirmation. Affirmations are goals rephrased as *positive, personalized statements that fuel goal attainment.* They make your goal statements much more powerful because they tend to more effectively penetrate the subconscious mind, which, scientists say, drives about 80 percent of what we do.

It has been known for decades that our minds have a conscious component, which interprets messages sent to it by the five senses, and a subconscious component, which is the storehouse of memories, habits, self-image, and beliefs. *Interestingly, the subconscious mind cannot tell the difference between truth and fantasy.* It accepts as truth everything the conscious mind tells it. If the conscious mind, which interprets what your five senses take in, has been telling your unconscious mind nonsense for years, such as "You cannot improve certain skills that are important to you," "You cannot cope under certain circumstances," "Some of the things you want are just out of your league," and so on, you will act in a manner consistent with this negative, self-limiting programming. Garbage in, garbage out. Instead, you can change the messages your subconscious tells you and tap its power to attain your goals.

Affirmations capitalize on two facts: first, the subconscious mind accepts as fact anything you tell it, and second, statements phrased in positive terms, in the first person, and in the present tense penetrate the subconscious more readily.

Given these facts, the value of changing your goals into affirmations should be apparent. Here's how to do it. Using our three previous goal statements, we'll convert each one into an affirmation.

Goal: "This quarter, I will hire three marketing representatives with e-commerce experience."

Affirmation: "This quarter, I am hiring three of the best marketing representatives with outstanding e-commerce experience."

Goal: "This month, I will meet with my top three customers to determine their product and service needs for the coming year."

Affirmation: "This month, I am meeting with my top three customers and determining their product and service needs for the coming year. I am providing outstanding service."

Goal: "By the end of this quarter, I will identify three tasks that regularly take up my time and delegate them to Jim and Barbara, enabling me to take on more strategic projects."

Affirmation: "By the end of the month, I have identified three tasks that regularly take up my own time and have delegated them to my two 'up and comers,' Jim and Barbara. As a result, I am enabled to take on more strategic projects."

In examining the goal/affirmation statements, some readers may ask, "I don't get it, what's the difference?" The difference at the conscious level is very subtle. But at the subconscious level, you have left no doubt whatsoever what you want to achieve. Affirmations are goals stated in the first person, in the present tense, using positive language. Using the words "I will" suggests hesitation. You're telling your subconscious mind that there is a degree of doubt. Writing (and saying) "I am" is much more powerful. You're telling yourself that you are in the process of accomplishing the goal. In fact, I personally like to use language that is future-oriented, such as "I *have*" accomplished the goal. It becomes a done deed. That's my own preference, though you should use what works best for you. Just make sure you don't use negative language. Instead of saying "I will not fail," say "I am succeeding." Say, "I am calm, confident, and poised" rather than "I will not get angry."

Take a few minutes to try this technique. Begin by identifying a goal pertaining to your situation. Write it as a goal statement *first* (be sure to use your SMART criteria). Then, using the affirmation criteria (first person, present tense, positive language), convert each goal into an affirmation. The affirmation should not be substantively different from the goal. I remember reviewing a set of affirmations by one of my clients, only to discover that the goal, when converted into an affirmation, had little resemblance to the original! The goal does not change, it is simply rephrased.

Affirmations do not have to be attached to a specific goal statement. They can be generally inspirational as well. One person who attended a "Power of Positive Thinking in Business" workshop later told me she had created three sets of affirmations: for work, for herself, and for others (her children). For "self," she created the affirmation "I am a strong, confident, secure woman. I am accomplishing great things." She also developed one for her children that she tells them on a regular basis: "You are smart, capable, and courteous kids. You can do anything you put your mind to." Like you, I have developed two or three business-related affirmations focusing on delighting customers, taking good care of employees, and maintaining profitability. I limit my business affirmations to not more than three. Although three is not a magic number, too many affirmations can be distracting. I have also created affirmations on a personal level. The most powerful affirmation I have ever used is one that comes from the Bible: "I can do all things through Christ which strengtheneth me." I wrote it on a small index card after reading about it in Dr. Peale's bestseller *The Power of Positive Thinking*. That was almost twenty years ago. In the top drawer of my desk is that same index card, now yellowed and dog-eared from the passage of time. But its power to transform, motivate, and compel me to action has not diminished in any way. No matter what your religious affiliation is, I strongly recommend creating affirmations that bring meaning and power to your core belief system. Use them for your spouse, children, friends, coworkers, whomever you feel needs them.

Managers don't use affirmations enough. They assume that people already know how they feel about them. We know when a manager disapproves of our actions, because negative behaviors always get attention. Positive behaviors are rarely reinforced, other than an occasional "Good job." Try it out. Think of someone who has done a great job for you and write an affirmation. Here's an example: "Stephanie, I just wanted to tell you that I think you are an outstanding IS [information services] manager, and I really appreciate how hard you work and how well you manage your team. Thanks for being there for me!"

Practice saying your personal affirmations to yourself too, or out loud if you're alone — anytime, anyplace. The more you say them, the better the result you can expect. To make sure you don't forget to say your affirmations, link when you say them to an activity or a certain time of day (for example, taking your shower, opening your refrigerator, driving to work, booting up your computer, morning coffee break). Create visuals by writing them on Post-it Notes and affixing them in an obvious spot. One supervisor I know tapes them to her computer monitor. Try to get into the habit of repeating them at least two to three times a day, every day. It takes discipline, but I can personally attest to the power of this method. I cannot think of a time when it has failed me, and I've been using it for almost two decades. Keep in mind, though, that affirmations are not like having some kind of a genie in a magic lamp—they may not make you an NBA champion overnight (especially if you're five feet tall and over fifty!), but they can help you achieve your goals using your God-given talents.

As mentioned, affirmations are more powerful than goal statements. But we can further strengthen their positive effects when we combine them with visualization.

VISUALIZATION

Professional athletes and most successful businesspeople visualize regularly. As reported in a *Wall Street Journal* article, today's most successful business executives attribute their success to six activities, visualization being one of them: "They are able to transcend their previous levels of accomplishment. They avoid the so-called comfort zone, that no-man's-land where an employee feels too much at home. They do what they do for the art of it and are guided by compelling, internal goals. They solve problems rather than place blame. They confidently take risks after laying out the worst consequences beforehand, and *they are able to rehearse coming actions or events mentally*" (italics mine). The article goes on to say, "Top chief executives imagined every facet and feeling of what would have to happen to make a presentation a success, practicing a kind of purposeful daydreaming. A less effective executive would prepare his facts and agendas but not his psyche."

Without this playing with fantasy no work has ever yet
come to birth. The debt we owe to the play of
imagination is incalculable.

—CARL JUNG, PSYCHOTHERAPIST

Just as you can benefit from monitoring and controlling your self-talk, you can benefit from monitoring and controlling the images that appear in your imagination. A professional golfer visualizes the shot he is about to make landing precisely in the spot desired. A professional salesperson visualizes herself making a successful sales call. A business executive visualizes a flawless presentation to the board of directors. In all cases, they see themselves succeeding in their imaginations and later, in the actual event, find themselves almost automatically playing out what they imagined. A sports psychologist, Terry Orlick, offers the following visualization points in his book *In Pursuit of Excellence:* "With performance imagery your ultimate goal is to draw on all your senses to feel yourself executing skills perfectly. This allows a slight firing of the neural pathways that are actually involved in the performance of these skills. It can be viewed as a way of programming your circuits. What you are trying to do is to program a positive performance into your brain and nervous system so that you will free your body to follow. Imagery helps to establish a positive performance pattern. It also can strengthen self-confidence and help you believe that you can perform in a real situation, in the manner of which you are capable."

An executive of a *Fortune* 500 company once told me that he had applied this technique when attempting to become a black belt in karate. The test included splitting a board in half using his hand. "No matter how hard I tried," he said, "I could not split that board in half. It was frustrating because I knew I had the physical strength to do it. So I went to my karate teacher and asked him what I was doing wrong. This was his reply: 'Reenact in your mind your attempt at splitting the board in half and tell me what you see in your mind.' " The executive replied, "My hand is moving towards the surface of the board at the right speed and in the right position, and just before it reaches the board, there's a sudden hesitation, and bang, I smash my hand, nearly breaking my knuckles and wrist." The teacher asked,

"What are you thinking when you hesitate?" The executive replied, "I'm thinking, 'Ooh, this is going to hurt!' "

Here's what the teacher suggested: "I want you to close your eyes and visualize your hand going right *through* the board. Feel your hand passing through the wood like butter. Hear the wood splintering, and feel the exhilaration and euphoria of your accomplishment." The executive said he did exactly what he was told and on the first try smashed the board in half—with absolutely no pain. He told me he has applied this visualization technique in the business setting with equal success. What is your board? Are you pulling back because you see and fear the worst, or are you seeing a successful way through?

> *Formulate and stamp indelibly on your mind a picture of*
> *yourself as succeeding. Hold this picture tenaciously. Never*
> *permit it to fade. Your mind will seek to develop this picture.*
> *Never think of yourself as failing; Never doubt the reality*
> *of the mental image. That is most dangerous, for the*
> *mind always tries to complete what it pictures.*
> —Dr. Norman Vincent Peale

Perhaps the most important point to remember in visualization is *never* to see yourself failing in your imagination. *Always see yourself performing perfectly.*

How to Visualize Success

Positive visualization is easy. You can use it to prepare for a meeting, a sales call, an important presentation—any situation in business that is important to you. Here are four simple steps:

1. **Quiet your mind.** Find a quiet place where you can relax and close your eyes for at least several minutes.
2. **Imagine yourself performing perfectly in the upcoming situation.** Visualize others responding to you as you believe they are likely to respond if you say and do the things you imagine to be ideal.
3. **Engage as many senses as possible in your imagination.** See vivid details of everything around you, hear all the sounds from

voices to chairs squeaking to the wall clock ticking. See the people around you sitting in their places, feel the carpeting under your feet and your hands on the table in front of you, smell the aroma of coffee, and so on.

4. **Replay the actual event after its completion.** Address any weaknesses in your performance. In your imagination replay those portions where you faltered, seeing and feeling a perfect performance.

Through visualization, you build a storehouse of successful experiences by *seeing* what you want already in your possession (being the managing director, winning the contract, or whatever). It's like directing a movie in your mind. Who is with you? Where are you, and what do you see? How do you look? What do you hear? View the scene from above, front, behind, left, and right. Zoom in and out. Everything should be ideal, perfect. Home run champ Mark McGwire was interviewed by *The New York Times* after hitting seventy home runs during the 1998 baseball season, beating the previous record held by Roger Maris. The interviewer asked Mark, "How did you do it?" He indicated that he had used the visualization technique. The fascinating part of the story is what he chose to visualize. Some think he probably visualized the ball sailing out of the park. In fact, during the interview he said, "I visualized my bat making contact with the ball." That's it! I guess Mark figured that all he had to do was make contact at the right spot on the bat with the ball and his mighty swing would take care of the rest.

Everyone has been motivated by some incident or story that at one time or another has made a lasting impression on his or her thinking. Dr. Peale tells an incredible story about the power of visualization:

A famous trapeze performer had a group of students, young people who were ambitious to become performing stars. The class went through all the lesser stunts. Now the time came for each to perform on the high bar. All but one got through this test satisfactorily. But the last aspirant looked up at the bar, and at once a negative self-image took over and he visualized the worst: one slip, and he would fall to the ground. He froze. He could not move a muscle. His imagination was

effectively blocking off the knowledge he had gained of the proce-
dure. Terrified, the boy stammered, "I can't. I cannot do it. I see myself
falling. I just cannot do it."

"If I did not know you were capable, I wouldn't ask you to do this,"
said the older man. "Look, I'll tell you how. First throw your heart over
that bar up there, and your body will follow." He meant, of course, to
"throw" faith, confidence, and an achievement over the difficulty—
and the material part would follow naturally.

It was wise advice. The boy's thinking unfroze. He changed his
mental image and finally passed his test without incident.

Everyone faces crises. By anticipating the worst we tend to freeze
and become unable to function properly. But by imaging—throwing
mind and heart over an obstacle—the obstacle can be overcome.
The result inevitably follows the direction of the mind.

Part Three

THE ENERGIZING POWER

6

The Ten Traits of a Positive Thinker

When I joined the Peale Center to develop the "Power of Positive Thinking in Business" workshop, I assembled a team to research the works of Dr. Peale. We had plenty of material to work with. During the course of his lifetime, he had written more than forty-five books and thousands of sermons, articles, and pamphlets. We also had access to the hundreds of videos and cassettes he had produced. Our challenge was not finding enough material but rather how we would make sense of and organize the huge volume of material at our disposal. It was especially important to identify the key concepts that would apply to business. After about fourteen months of culling through and analyzing the material, a pattern emerged. Dr. Peale characterized positive thinkers as possessing a variety of positive attributes. These attributes or traits were scattered through the volumes of material he had written. There were dozens of them. Using an "affinity" process, were sorted the traits into groups and labeled them based on their overall concept or theme. What emerged was a set of ten positive innate traits. Positive traits are inborn characteristics (physical, mental, emotional, or spiritual) that contribute to one's level of success. The ten traits of a positive thinker are optimism, enthusiasm, belief, integrity, courage, confidence, determination, patience, calmness, and focus.

You can probably imagine how incredibly successful you would be if you had high levels of all these traits and applied them appropriately. If you, like many others, think that only certain people are courageous, confident, or enthusiastic, you'd better think again. The fact is, we were all *born* with the ten traits of a positive thinker. However, in nearly all of us these innate traits have been covered up to varying degrees by negative conditioning. A once optimistic child comes to view the world more pessimistically after his optimism and enthusiasm are repeatedly met with negativity. "Stop that, you'll get hurt!" "Why can't you be more like your sister?" "How many times do I have to show you how to do this? You're hopeless!" "Go ahead and try, you'll never make it." "You're a quitter!" "You've let us down again." These are just a few examples of the kinds of negative messages many people have experienced over the years—and, to their detriment, taken to heart. Messages like these eventually shape our beliefs about the ten traits. We come to believe that we either possess them (or some combination of them) or not. What happens is that the traits, to varying degrees, become dulled or, in some cases, dormant. They no longer operate freely within us as they did at a very young age.

Dr. Denis Waitley writes, "Champions are born and then unmade by their perceptions and responses. Losers are not born to lose. They are made that way by what they perceive and choose." There's a true story about a man who walked into a tattoo shop. As he entered the shop, he noticed a big, burly, rough-looking guy in a sleeveless shirt walking out. And there across his muscular arms was the inscription "BORN TO LOSE." In amazement, the man asked the storeowner, "Why would anybody want a permanent tattoo on their body that says, 'BORN TO LOSE'?" The storeowner replied, "It's simple: tattoo on mind, tattoo on arm." In other words, he suggested that if the man had an indelible imprint of losing burned into his mind, his actions would follow suit. In a way, losing becomes a self-fulfilling prophecy.

THE TEN TRAITS OF A POSITIVE THINKER DEFINED

A psychological study was conducted by the Peale Center that resulted in the following definitions of the ten traits. I recommend that before you read the definitions, first think of how you would define them and then compare your definition with these.

- **Optimism:** *A belief in and expectation of positive outcomes, even in the face of difficulty, challenge, or crisis*
- **Enthusiasm:** *Having high levels of interest, positive energy, passion, or personal motivation*
- **Belief:** *Trusting in oneself, others, and/or a higher spiritual power to provide support and guidance when needed*
- **Integrity:** *Acting on a personal commitment to honesty, openness, and fairness; living by and for one's standards*
- **Courage:** *The willingness to take risks and overcome fears, even when the outcome is uncertain*
- **Confidence:** *Being personally assured of one's abilities, capabilities, and potential*
- **Determination:** *The tireless pursuit of a goal, purpose, or cause*
- **Patience:** *The willingness to wait for opportunity, readiness, or results from oneself and others*
- **Calmness:** *Maintaining serenity and seeking balance daily in response to difficulty, challenge, or crisis; taking time to reflect and think*
- **Focus:** *Attention directed through the setting of goals and priorities*

THE POSITIVE THINKING INVENTORY

As mentioned, all ten traits are innate; however, they have been concealed, to varying degrees, by our negative programming and influences. Fortunately, you can *consciously* call up these traits whenever you need them.

The first step in rediscovering and reactivating the ten traits is to determine where you stand relative to them. That is, to what degree on a regular basis are you optimistic, patient, confident, and so on? The Positive Thinking Inventory was developed over several years by a psychometrist to gauge the frequency with which people engage in positive thinking. Simply put, a psychometrist's job is to measure the immeasurable. On the surface, a trait such as determination seems like an intangible quality, but the psychometrist was able to identify specific, measurable behavioral characteristics or indicators for each of the ten traits. Working with outside scholars, instructional designers, and members of the Peale Center, the psychometrist generated up to fifteen behavioral indicators for each trait, recognizing that some had stronger correlation to their respective traits than others did. An inventory was developed and underwent extensive reliability and validity testing. Reliability refers to the accuracy and consistency of a test or inventory over time, while validity refers to whether or not the test or inventory actually measures what it purports to. Eventually, certain indicators were eliminated, while others were kept because of the strength of the correlation. As a result, five behavioral indicators per trait, with statistically significant correlation coefficients, were selected as a basis for the Positive Thinking Inventory. It is not a perfect test—in fact, there's no such thing. All tests of this nature are in a "state of becoming." They improve over time. Hundreds of people have taken the inventory that you are about to take and have attested to its accuracy. As you prepare to take the test, keep in mind that there is a total of fifty statements (items) that describe the thoughts and behaviors of positive thinking. You will not know which trait they pertain to until *after* you have completed the test. This is to avoid bias. Please follow the rating instructions, and be as candid and straightforward as you can; these are not meant to be trick questions.

My advice is to go with your first instinct. Don't try to read too much into or out of a question. Instead, go with your interpretation of the question and respond with your initial reaction regarding how these apply to you.

The Positive Thinking Inventory

On a piece of paper, indicate how frequently you engage in the thought, feeling, or action described in each statement by rating it from 0 to 5.

5: Almost always	2: Sometimes
4: Most of the time	1: Almost never
3: Usually	0: Not relevant; not sure

Statement	0–5

1. I know there is a power beyond myself from which I can draw strength.
2. I am committed to living my life to high standards and a higher purpose.
3. I don't let my mistakes discourage me.
4. I allow people time to reach their own solutions.
5. I have the quality of being able to stick to plans and projects.
6. I see individual events as part of a greater plan.
7. I don't let danger or crisis paralyze me.
8. I keep control over my emotions.
9. I tell the truth.
10. I don't let doubt affect my pursuit of a worthy goal.
11. I rise to the occasion when goals seem out of reach.
12. I keep my eye on my goals, even through daily distractions.
13. I speak up on behalf of unpopular positions if I think they have merit.
14. I use the same standard of measuring my own behavior as the behavior of others.
15. I make a conscious effort to react evenly.
16. I wake up feeling excited about the day ahead.
17. I react to stress with self-control.
18. I thrive on finding needs that interest me and fulfilling them.
19. I stay in touch with my goals.
20. I take on assignments that interest me even when the odds of a favorable outcome are slim.
21. I meet challenges with a sense of control.
22. I stay on course even when things get uncertain.

23. I make sure fear and feelings of inferiority don't drive my actions.

24. I don't allow anxiety over an outcome to rattle my composure.

25. I concentrate my energy where it will do the most good.

26. I am able to control my worries and resentments.

27. I summon up the energy needed to see a job through.

28. I act with a sense of hope about what lies ahead.

29. I contribute to the group's morale even under difficult circumstances.

30. I practice affirming myself in my skills and my outlook.

31. I show energy about projects that excite others.

32. I create a mental plan to get a task done.

33. I move forward decisively.

34. I have a clear picture of where I want to be in my life.

35. I don't obsess over an issue.

36. I work to minimize the impact of my doubts and fears.

37. I don't act or speak hastily without considering the consequences.

38. I don't cop out hoping others will get the job done.

39. I avoid gossiping about others.

40. I gear myself to be positively hopeful in my attitudes and expectations.

41. I keep my spirits up even when things aren't going well.

42. I don't allow worry to get the best of me.

43. I'm not from the "let's just be done with it" school of fast solutions.

44. I'm energetic in pursuing outcomes.

45. I engage in those activities that are necessary to meet my goals.

46. I get a kick out of life.

47. I treat people evenhandedly and fairly.

48. I do not allow my fears to set my goals.

49. I don't engage in playing off one person against another.

50. I do not panic when adversity occurs.

SCORING THE INVENTORY

To determine your score on each of the positive thinking traits, consult the list of traits below. On your piece of paper, record your response for each of the five statements that correspond to each positive thinking trait. (For example, statements 21, 28, 36, 40, and 41 describe the thoughts and behaviors found in those exhibiting optimism.) Once you record your responses, add up the five responses to get a total score for each of the ten traits. Go ahead and score your inventory now; then I will discuss how to extract useful meaning from it.

Optimism: 21, 28, 36, 40, 41
Enthusiasm: 16, 18, 31, 44, 46
Belief: 1, 2, 6, 30, 42
Integrity: 9, 14, 39, 47, 49
Courage: 7, 13, 20, 22, 29
Confidence: 3, 10, 17, 23, 33
Determination: 5, 11, 27, 32, 38
Patience: 4, 15, 24, 37, 43
Calmness: 8, 26, 35, 48, 50
Focus: 12, 19, 25, 34, 45

Example

Optimism
   21: 2
   28: 1
   36: 3
   40: 3
   41: 5
Total: 14

INTERPRETING THE RESULTS

In interpreting your results, here are few tips on what to look for.

Which trait(s) scored higher than you had expected?

Any total trait score of 20 or above would be considered high-scoring. Any item scoring above 3 also would be considered high-scoring. We sometimes underestimate our strengths. This could be due to the fact that some of us are not aware of what they are or perhaps do not receive direct feedback on them from others. Were there any unexpected results? How would you explain a higher-than-expected score?

Which trait(s) scored lower than you expected?

Any total trait score below 19 should be investigated further. Any item scoring lower than 3 should also be looked into. Most of us are pretty hard on ourselves, so there aren't usually too many surprises relative to lower-than-expected scores on the traits. I have found that most people are fairly modest and don't want to think of themselves too highly. On the other hand, I do recommend paying particular attention to scores that are lower than expected.

More important, I suggest that you identify specific low-scoring items and reread them to see if you interpreted them accurately. If you did, ask yourself, "Is this really true about myself, or is it an incorrect perception?"

Identify traits with a large degree of variation. Let's say, as an example, that you scored the following on "confidence":

3: 5
10: 2
17: 4
23: 5
33: 1
Total: 17

The range of variation is 1 to 5, whereas in other traits you might have seen all 4s and 5s. My recommendation is to review the high items (3, 17, 23) and the low items (10, 33) by rereading the respective questions. Then compare the similarities and differences between the high- and low-scoring questions. For instance, the question for item 3, which scored a 5, reads, "I don't let my mistakes discourage me." Meanwhile, the question for item 33, "I move forward decisively," scored a 1. Both items are strongly correlated to the "confidence" trait, but how do you explain the variation between them? One possible explanation is that although you do not allow mistakes to discourage you, they may make you more *hesitant*, which might explain why you do not move ahead as decisively as you would like. There may be any number of explanations, but since you know yourself better than anybody else does, your instinct is probably a reliable indicator of the most accurate explanation.

360-DEGREE FEEDBACK

Most self-assessments, such as the Positive Thinking Inventory, are subject to bias. It is difficult for us to be objective when evaluating ourselves. For the greatest accuracy, I recommend 360-degree feedback. Ideally, you would identify several people in your organization who would complete an inventory based on *their* perception of you. I suggest your boss, one or two coworkers, and one or two direct reports. You can decide for yourself whether the culture in your organization is conducive to the kind of openness required for honest 360-degree feedback. Once the inventories are completed and scored, look for gaps among the respondents' scores, including your own. Based on those gaps (and there will be gaps!), organize one-on-one meetings with the other respondents to collect more *qualitative* data. Try to get more specific information from them.

For example, one very bright woman with a promising career in a large organization scored herself very low on confidence. But to her surprise, others scored her very high. With disbelief, she asked her evaluators why they had scored her so high on confidence, when she had scored herself so low. I was present when a direct report told her, "You started working in this company as a secretary and have worked your way up to a management level position. You always seem sure of yourself, and you've been a tremendous inspiration to me." The manager sat in stunned silence, her eyes glistening. She didn't know what to say. Later, she told me privately, "I had no idea that people thought of me as a confident person. I always thought of myself as insecure and lacking confidence." She, like many of us, often does not feel secure and confident *inside* but is able to exude it on the *outside*. She would not have known that had she not sought feedback from others. Keep in mind, however, that 360-degree feedback on the ten traits requires trust between you and the respondents. You will be vulnerable to a certain extent. You are sharing information that is very personal.

I have seen this technique work very effectively in high-trust environments. I recall one five-member work group debriefing the Positive Thinking Inventory. They were incredibly supportive of one another, sharing their insights and recommendations. Each person revealed which trait area he or she wanted to improve the most. One gentleman, known for his quick temper, was affectionately nicknamed "Mr. Calmness." He knew his temper was getting the best of him and earnestly wanted to do something about it. His team rallied around him and over time helped him to live up to his nickname. He became changed forever.

Although we're talking about applying positive thinking in the workplace, I recommend you also ask your spouse, a friend, your significant other, or some other person close to you to complete the inventory. It may reveal different things. For one, we may have two completely different personae, one at the office, the other at home. You may be very enthusiastic at home (especially on weekends) but not very enthusiastic at the office. On the other hand, you may be very determined at the office (meeting deadlines, accomplishing tasks) but not very determined at home. Feedback from those we are closest to outside the work environment can be very revealing. My wife, Catherine, and I both completed two copies of the inventory, one on ourselves, the other on our perceptions of each other. Going through them revealed some interesting gaps and led to a constructive discussion on why we perceived each other the way we did. People we are close to have the depth of knowledge about us to provide greater insights into our behavior. All in all, the inventory will provide you with an idea of your trait levels on a per trait basis and can serve as a benchmark for measuring your progress. Although it's not a perfect instrument, it is a very good guide.

SITUATIONAL POSITIVE THINKING

Invariably, what you will discover is that we exude varying degrees of the traits, depending on the *circumstances* or *situation*. Remember, we all possess the traits innately. Most people taking the inventory think that all low scores are "bad" and all high scores are "good" and therefore that the objective is to move from low to high. But that's not what I'm promoting. Let me ask you: Do you think it's possible to have *too much* of a given trait?

REGULATING YOUR TRAITS

It is very possible to go overboard, with negative consequences. For example, too much enthusiasm can be perceived as being shallow or insincere. On the other hand, too little enthusiasm can be interpreted as being dull and uninterested. All of the traits you can apply in a given situation should be regulated based on:

1. Your knowledge of yourself
2. Your knowledge of the other individual(s) involved
3. The specific situation

The following case makes this point.

Bob, a salesperson, has just completed his first meeting with a high-potential prospect. He steps into the elevator and says to himself, "Before I even went in there, I knew I would blow their doors off. Man, was I outstanding! At first they acted like a bunch of cold fish, but I had them in hysterics by the time I walked out. They absolutely loved my video and brochures. I've got this account wrapped. I know I do. And I did it in just over half an hour. Enthusiasm sells! Time to take a little break and reward myself."

Meanwhile, back in the conference room, the three people Bob met with (the vice president of manufacturing and two managers) are getting up from their chairs, having decided not to do business with Bob or his company. After Bob left the room, the VP remarked, "Yeah, we'll get back to him, all right. In my twenty-two years of meeting with salespeople, I've met more than a few showboats, but this guy Bob came as close as anyone to being tossed out on his ear. What a presumptuous, cocky little so-and-so. He asked us all of two questions and launched right into his shtick." One of the managers added, "The guy acted like he must have had six cups of coffee before coming in here. I know that's what it would take to get me so wired." The other manager closed the discussion with "Let's keep looking. I think he's got a good product, but I don't like his style."

Like all of us, Bob has the ten traits of a positive thinker, but in the preceding example some of the traits operated at levels where they did more harm than good, and others, which would have benefited him, were not even in the picture. Of the ten traits, which ones did Bob appear to overuse? Which ones could he have benefited by, and how? You might say that he overdid it on enthusiasm and confidence, while he could have used more patience and calmness. Men in particular habitually use only a small part of the power they possess and might use in the appropriate circumstances.

How Much Is Too Much or Too Little?

You can both overdo and underdo each of the traits to your detriment. Here are examples for each trait.

Too Much	Trait	Too Little
Pollyannaish, unrealistic	**Optimism**	Negative, pessimistic
Insincere, phony	**Enthusiasm**	Dull, uninterested
Dogmatic, fanatical	**Belief**	Vacillating, indecisive
Self-righteous, judgmental	**Integrity**	Unethical, shady
Foolish, having poor judgment	**Courage**	Cowardly, spineless
Arrogant, smug	**Confidence**	Insecure, weak
Stubborn, uncompromising	**Determination**	Quitter, giving up easily
Indecisive, pushover	**Patience**	Hasty, rash
Lazy, unmotivated	**Calmness**	Quick-tempered, fidgety
Narrow-minded, myopic	**Focus**	Scattered, disorganized

Factors to Consider When Regulating Positive Thinking Traits

There are four factors to consider when regulating your positive thinking traits in any situation, much like a pilot regulates the flight of a plane by selecting and turning certain dials on a control panel:

1. "What's the weather like?" or what is the work situation you are going into: giving bad news, handling conflict, managing change, asking for a promotion, and so on.
2. "What's the destination?" or what is your desired outcome.
3. "Which instruments do I use now?" or what is the best trait or combination of traits to call up, based on your knowledge of your trait level (as determined through the Positive Thinking Inventory) and your assessment of the other person(s) involved.
4. "How much should I turn this dial, and in what direction?" or what are the appropriate trait levels? Given your knowledge of yourself and the other person(s) involved, you need to set the proper level (turn the dial) on each of the traits pertinent to achieving the desired outcome.

Knowing which traits to regulate and by how much can be determined by comparing your expected versus actual inventory scores. *Example:*

ACTUAL SCORE	HIGH	LOW
EXPECTED SCORE		
High	Optimism, enthusiasm determination	Belief, integrity, confidence
Low	Courage, patience	Calmness, focus

Here are some guidelines for interpreting and dealing with traits that fall into certain quadrants of the matrix.

High–High

This is a good place to be! It suggests that you know yourself well and were not surprised by your results. If nothing else, it reaffirmed what you already suspected. It may suggest that you have nurtured and reinforced those areas over time. Knowing this tells you that your traits are more available and evident in your day-to-day interactions. What you should watch for is a tendency to overdo one or more of them. Because this comes so naturally, it's easy to do. Be especially watchful when dealing with certain people and situations that warrant a ratcheting down of those behaviors. For instance, if you are giving a status report to your boss on a project that is over budget and overdue and he happens to eschew spirited, happy-go-lucky types, you would be well advised to tone your enthusiasm down.

Since you will probably view the situation optimistically, you would want to consider adjusting it down and turn up your focus, which, according to the matrix, was low. He will appreciate your sticking to the facts and proposing realistic strategies to deal with the issues.

High–Low

A "high–low" designation means that although you thought you were high in certain trait areas, you were actually low. It suggests that you may not exude as much confidence as you think you do. In this case, you need to turn the dial up regardless of the person or situation. In some situations, you might need to turn it up significantly. For example, if you are announcing cost-cutting measures due to a projected shortfall in company revenues for the next two quarters, you'll need a high dose of *belief* (you're taking the proper measures under the circumstances), *integrity* (everybody will receive accurate, timely information, and the cost-cutting measures will be fair to all, regardless of rank or tenure in the company), and *confidence* (believing that things will turn around, as the company is strong, with capable leadership, and so forth).

Low–High

In this case you are more courageous and patient than you thought. The only danger is that there may have been times when, in an effort to compensate for your perceived weaknesses in these areas, you overcompensated. I suggest trying to explain gaps for traits falling into the "low–high" area. Earlier in this chapter, I shared a story of a manager who perceived herself as being unconfident, when in reality she was perceived as a very confident person. One possible explanation for the gap in perception is that she may not have received acknowledgment from people important to her. There are many people who, because they do not receive feedback or reinforcement from significant people in their life, are unaware that they possess certain positive traits.

Low–Low

The good news is that you know where your weak areas are and can focus on improving them. It also means that you'll need to work extra hard to "raise the bar" on the trait(s) falling into this quadrant, which in this case are calmness and focus. A "low–low" designation may indicate that you have had problems with those particular traits all your life. Chances are that they spill over into your personal life as well. This is what I call a "chronic" area: you know you are weak in a certain area but have not taken measures to change. A specific action plan should be developed to improve these areas, followed by diligent adherence to the plan. In the next section, I'll address specific strategies for "operationalizing" the traits.

"ACT AS IF"

There are two ways to "reactivate" dormant traits. One way is to rethink how we view the traits on a personal level. So, for instance, if you believe that you can't be enthusiastic or confident, you probably can't—because your beliefs about the trait(s) will affect your thinking, which affects your feelings, which ultimately affect your actions or behaviors. I remember dealing with a gentleman who was an eighteen-year veteran with one of my client companies. The Positive Thinking Inventory revealed—or rather, reaffirmed—that this man lacked enthusiasm. He said, "[The result] doesn't surprise me. I've been this way all my life. I don't think I can ever change." He's right. If he doesn't think he'll ever change, he won't. In his case, though, his job depended on it. Apparently, his supervisor had brought to his attention the fact that his lack of enthusiasm was having a negative effect on his team. He lacked "zip" when dealing with his direct reports.

Happily, though, over a period of several months after taking the inventory, he rediscovered his own unique version of enthusiasm.

You see, he had been comparing himself to the Richard Simmons type of personality—perpetually energetic and happy. During our meetings, he came to realize that "enthusiasm" manifests itself behaviorally in many different ways. The key was to find which way would work best for his overall "low-key" personality. So instead of overcompensating by becoming overly expressive, he simply concentrated on allowing his natural enthusiasm to come forth instead of suppressing it.

Sometimes, no matter how much we try to reframe our thinking, we are not persuaded. I am reminded of a popular commercial appearing nationally in the late 1990s. It featured a shipping and receiving clerk on the phone with a customer who is apparently making impossible demands. The clerk confidently, without any hesitation, tells the customer, "I can do that, I can do that, Yes, I can do that." Then, after hanging up, he looks up with fear in his eyes. "How am I going to do that?"

Even though he didn't *feel* confident, he had to *act* that way in front of the customer. This is where the "act as if" technique comes in handy. Recall that in an earlier chapter I talked about the B-T-F-A chain, in which our beliefs drive our thoughts, which drive our feelings, which result in certain behaviors. With the "act as if" technique, the B-T-F-A chain can be worked in reverse: A-F-T-B. This proven technique is based on the fact that if you simply *act* a particular way, you will soon *think, feel,* and *believe* as one for whom the action feels comfortable and normal. For example, one of the greatest fears businesspeople suffer is the fear of public speaking. And for some people, all the positive self-talk in the world won't get them up in front of an audience or keep their knees from shaking uncontrollably when they do. Applying "act as if" helps override their belief system: you don't think about making the presentation, you just get out there and do it. By simply resolving to *act* like a supremely confident person, you quickly acquire the *feeling* of increased confidence. This feeling of confidence automatically triggers positive thoughts, such as "I can do this." By thinking you can succeed, you vastly improve the odds that you will be successful. Your success, over time, then helps to establish the *belief* that you are competent at making presentations, and consequently you feel confident doing so. The effectiveness of this simple technique was proven by Dr. William James at Harvard University decades ago. Today, it is often referred to as "fake it till you make it." Let me add a caution, though: I am not suggesting that you fake integrity or sincerity. Your intentions must be sincere and genuine. And eventually, with practice and repetition, you will no longer have to fake a trait because you will have overridden your conscious and subconscious belief system. Simply by resolving to act like a supremely confident person, you can quickly acquire a feeling of increased confidence.

THE INTERRELATIONSHIP AMONG BELIEFS, THOUGHTS, FEELINGS, ACTIONS, AND THE TEN TRAITS

When viewed as a cycle, we can see the relationship among beliefs, thoughts, feelings, and actions. We can jump in at any point and see how one feeds into the other. For example, a feeling of courage is likely to lead to an action that is timely, direct, and admirable. The outcome of the action provides input into the person's beliefs (about himself, others, and the world in which he operates). If the action is successful, the beliefs that gave rise to the thought(s), which led to the feeling of courage, will be reinforced. If the action is unsuccessful, those beliefs may be questioned and adjusted. What is represented by the clockwise motion (see diagram on the next page) can work equally well in reverse. For example, when someone "acts as if" he possesses a positive trait, such as determination, this action alone can automatically prompt *feelings* of determination, which in turn can prompt *thoughts* of determination, which over time can shape the *belief* that one is a determined person.

Whether we go clockwise or counterclockwise, the objective is to get our beliefs into step with reality. When that happens, *we are positioned to perform at our best*.

Positive thinking patterns will:

- Increase your personal and organizational success, satisfaction, and achievement.

Beliefs That Are in Step with Reality Are Best

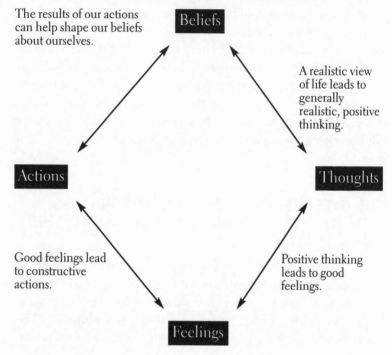

The results of our actions can help shape our beliefs about ourselves.

Beliefs

A realistic view of life leads to generally realistic, positive thinking.

Actions

Thoughts

Good feelings lead to constructive actions.

Positive thinking leads to good feelings.

Feelings

• Continually uncover and reinforce the ten traits of a positive thinker, all of which are innate.

The ten traits of a positive thinker exist in each and every one of us. We all have the capacity to reactivate the dormant ones and use them in tough situations to achieve positive outcomes.

7

Centering Power

In the previous chapter I discussed the ten traits of a positive thinker and how they can be reactivated to help you achieve extraordinary goals and objectives. You have already taken the first step to reactivating the traits by taking the Positive Thinking Inventory. As a result, you know which ones to focus on in a particular situation. Now I will go a step further and provide a thorough understanding of each trait, including specific techniques for awakening long-dormant traits, especially when circumstances warrant doing so.

The ten traits fall naturally into four distinct groups:

1. Centering Power
   - Belief
   - Integrity
   - Focus
2. Uplifting Power
   - Optimism
   - Enthusiasm
3. Driving Power
   - Confidence
   - Courage
   - Determination
4. Holding Power
   - Patience
   - Calmness

As you can see in the diagram below, the traits combine into natural groups relative to the planning and action stages of dealing with challenging situations. Centering Power is the power to get anchored before taking action, a planning stage. Uplifting Power is the power to energize ourselves in mind, body, and spirit as we move on to great things. Driving Power is the power of taking bold, decisive action. Holding Power is the power to maintain a steady, even disposition during a waiting period or when things get rough. These groupings are simply a guide and are not meant to fix any one trait exclusively into a particular stage of a situation. Any one of the traits can be effectively applied at any time. During the development of the Positive Thinking Inventory, we discovered that the traits correlated with one another to varying degrees. For instance, belief is strongly correlated with focus. If we are involved in a project that we strongly believe in, chances are we will maintain a strong focus on it until its completion. A strong, positive belief system drives integrity, and so on. Now let's address each trait on an individual basis in their respective groupings, starting with the Centering Power.

The "Powers" of Positive Thinking

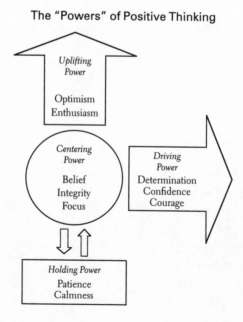

CENTERING POWER: BELIEF

Belief is trusting in oneself, others, and/or a higher spiritual power to provide support and guidance when needed.

Of all the traits, this is perhaps the most important—and the most controversial. It's the most important because every action begins with belief. It's extremely controversial in business because it includes the idea of a "higher spiritual power." Let's explore its meaning. The word "belief" derives from the Old English word *geléafa*, meaning "conviction that certain things are true."

We demonstrate belief each time we . . .

- Show a sureness or certainty that there is a power to draw upon to enhance our capabilities.
- Commit ourselves to live by a higher cause or purpose.
- Do not worry because it is contrary to having faith.
- Trust in an idea or system of principles.
- View single events as components of an overall plan or destiny.

BELIEF IN SELF

"If you don't stand for something, you'll fall for anything"; so go the lyrics of a country-western song I heard on the radio while driving one day. Sadly, there are many people today who don't know what they believe in. A good starting place is to believe in yourself. Success in business—or life, for that matter—depends on having a conviction that we possess a power deep inside to draw upon, a power that comes from the recognition that the human species, unlike any other species in the world, has the distinct capability to think, reason, and feel complex emotions. The enemy of belief in self is doubt. When the winds of doubt blow in, our thinking becomes scattered. We become confused and disoriented. We question our inherent worth as human beings. We are unable to make clear decisions and take decisive action.

Self-doubt creeps in when we lose sight of our individual identity and uniqueness. It attacks when we are most vulnerable, perhaps after suffering a series of personal and professional setbacks. It loves failure and tricks the mind into thinking that because a person has failed, he or she is a failure. I have seen this happen in people who lost their jobs, missed out on promotions, or simply missed accomplishing certain goals and objectives. People experiencing personal loss, such as divorce, are especially prone to self-doubt. Self-doubt leads to feelings of discouragement, despair, and self-pity. Self-doubt wreaks havoc in organizations because it can

- Lead to unethical behavior.
- Create mistrust.
- Prevent one from setting goals.
- Prevent one from achieving one's goals.
- Block other key traits (confidence, determination, courage, and more).

The only limit to our realization of tomorrow will be our doubts of today. Let us move forward with strong and active faith.
— FRANKLIN D. ROOSEVELT

It has been proven that strong doubt (to our detriment) or strong belief (to our good) can actually be an agent of biological change. Take the example of "Mr. Wright," whose story was recalled in a *New York Times* article:

In 1957, he was found to have cancer and was given only days to live. Hospitalized in Long Beach, Calif., with tumors the size of oranges, he heard that scientists had discovered a horse serum, Krebiozen, that appeared to be effective against cancer. He begged to receive it. His physician, Dr. Philip West, finally agreed and gave Mr. Wright an injection on a Friday afternoon. The following Monday, the astonished doctor found his patient out of his deathbed, joking with the nurses. The tumors, the doctor wrote later, "had melted like snowballs on a hot stove." Two months later, Mr. Wright read medical reports that the horse serum was a quack remedy. He immediately suffered a relapse. "Don't believe what you read in the papers," the doctor told Mr. Wright. Then he injected him with what he said was "a new super-refined double-strength" version of the drug. Actually, it was water, but again the tumor masses melted. Mr. Wright was "the picture of health" for another two months—until he read a definitive report stating that Krebiozen was worthless. He died two days later.

The article goes on to say, "Doctors who know the story dismiss it as one of those strange tales that medicine cannot explain. The idea that a patient's beliefs can make a fatal disease go away is hard to believe. But now scientists, as they learn that the placebo effect is even more powerful than anyone had been able to demonstrate, are also beginning to discover the biological mechanisms that cause it to achieve results that border on the miraculous. Using new techniques of brain imagery, they are uncovering a host of biological mechanisms that can turn a thought, belief, or desire into an agent of change in cells, tissues, and organs. They are learning that much of human perception is based not on information flowing into the brain from the outside world but what the brain, based on previous experience, expects to happen next."

You might say that in Mr. Wright's case, doubt led to poor health and his eventual demise, while belief led to healing and life. Simply put, our self-expectations are often a predictor of our success.

> *When you expect the best, you release a magnetic force in your mind which by law of attraction tends to bring the best to you. But if you expect the worst, you release from your mind the power of repulsion which tends to force the best from you. It is amazing how a sustained expectation of the best sets in motion forces which cause the best to materialize.*
> — DR. NORMAN VINCENT PEALE

In a sense, doubt includes belief. You can believe you're a failure or believe you're a success. Both involve belief; the difference is in the outcome.

BELIEF IN OTHERS

In the workplace we must often depend on others to reach our goals. What happens if we don't believe in or trust our coworkers? If we doubt ourselves, chances are that we will doubt and mistrust others. Mistrust is perhaps the greatest impediment to reaching interdependent goals. Some common symptoms of mistrust include:

- Hoarding information
- Working secretively

- Not sharing ideas
- Failure to delegate

On the other hand, believing and trusting in others free us. They enable us to take on new and exciting projects that challenge and motivate us. It liberates those on the receiving end as well.

THE PYGMALION EFFECT

You may be familiar with the "Pygmalion effect," which describes the influence of self-fulfilling prophecy. Pygmalion was a mythical Greek sculptor who carved a statue of a beautiful woman. He literally worshiped the statue and wished it would come to life. According to the legend, the goddess Venus took pity on Pygmalion and brought the statue, Galitea, to life. Hence, the belief in something else, in this case a statue, caused it to come to life. The Pygmalion effect in business has been well researched and documented. It was most notably described in a classic 1988 *Harvard Business Review* article, "Pygmalion in Management," by J. Sterling Livingston. The research findings showed a strong relationship between managers' expectations and their subordinates' behavior and performance.

There's another classic example of positive self-expectancy, this time in an academic environment. Three teachers were told that because they were the three best teachers in their school, they would be rewarded with three classes of the brightest students in the school. At the end of the school year, the students taught by the three selected teachers scored 20 to 30 percent above the grade levels of the entire school. In fact, the names of the teachers and students who participated in this experiment had been pulled from a hat. The researcher concluded that the students had done so well because of the "law of positive expectancy," which is that *you achieve what you expect to achieve and what others expect you to achieve.* This classic experiment was conducted three hundred times with the same impressive results by Dr. Robert Rosenthal of Harvard University.

BELIEF IN A HIGHER SPIRITUAL POWER

Studies show that more than 75 percent of Americans believe in a higher spiritual power. But studies also show that most Americans are uncomfortable with the idea of mixing spirituality with business. The view is based on the idea that church and state should remain separate and that spirituality and religion are personal and have no business being brought into business. This was the most challenging and controversial issue I confronted when developing the workshop "The Power of Positive Thinking in Business." I did not want the program to be construed as a religious one because it is not. Therefore I made a conscious decision on two important issues that were at odds with each other. I wanted the program to clearly reflect the same heritage as the best-selling book *The Power of Positive Thinking*, which, as I've mentioned, was based on Judeo-Christian principles. But I also wanted to reach secular, mainstream businesspeople.

It seemed as though it would be impossible, for I was completely aware of the issues. In the early development of the program, a market research firm conducted focus groups around the country to test the idea of bringing a spiritually based program into the workplace. The results of the focus groups clearly indicated that there was little room for spirituality in business, for all the obvious reasons.

The results did not sway me from my desire to introduce positive thinking to the business community. It nevertheless led me to take a serious look at how to introduce the spiritual component of positive thinking. I grappled especially with how to include the notion of a higher spiritual power in a nonjudgmental, unbiased, inclusive manner. I could not eliminate it, for doing so would have removed the "power" behind positive thinking. I decided to include it, but in a way that would leave it up to each individual how to interpret and apply it in business. Interestingly enough, more than five years after the focus group study, we have discovered a tremendous wave of interest in spirituality in business. For instance, in the Fall 1999 issue of *Business Week*, the cover story headline read, "The Growing Presence of Spirituality in Corporate America—Religion in the Workplace." And the Summer 1999 issue of MIT's *Sloan Management Review* featured a comprehensive study of spirituality in the workplace. Both reflect the rising popularity of what seems to be a spiritual wave in business. Overall, they indicate that people in the workplace view themselves as complete human beings; you can't check your spirituality at the door.

The Higher Spiritual Power in Business

Reviewing the definition of "belief," notice that it includes the idea of "trusting in a higher spiritual power." What do I mean by that phrase? Naturally this applies only to those who subscribe to the idea of a higher power. For those to whom it does *not* apply, please refer back to the first half of the definition, "trusting in oneself, [and] others." But for the 75 percent or so to whom it does apply, I'd like to spend a few moments to flesh out some ideas on how to leverage the higher spiritual power in business *without* infringing on the rights of others.

Spirituality Versus Religion

In order to gain an understanding of how to tap into the higher spiritual power, it's important first to address the idea of spirituality and religion. Confusion between them abounds; in fact, many people use the terms interchangeably. Although I am not a theologian, I can tell you that while the two are obviously related, there are also some vast differences between them.

For example, you can practice religion without necessarily being spiritual (as a lifelong member of the Catholic Church, I can tell you that many of my fellow Catholics follow the teachings of the Church, right down to the letter of the law, but don't practice the spirit of the law). On the other hand, you can be a deeply spiritual person without subscribing to any organized religion. This would certainly apply, for instance, to many Native Americans. People in business, regardless of their religious affiliations, don't want religion imposed on them. Religion is a private matter and should be kept as such. Spirituality is different because it has universal meaning, crossing all religious and ethnic boundaries. Spirituality is derived from the Latin word *spiritus*, meaning "breath." According to *Merriam Webster's Dictionary*, it is a "life-giving force," or animating principle. Few people would argue that it's not important for an individual, groups, teams, or, for that matter, a corporation to have "spirit." The idea of exuding "spirit" in the workplace is accepted, if not welcomed, by most people. "Spirituality," however, has a deeper meaning and can perhaps cause some uneasiness because it involves the expression of spirit. Some people, when expressing themselves spiritually, may use religious terms or symbols in the process. When I was consulting with an openly evangelical Christian company in Texas, for example, it was not unusual to hear someone shout out "Praise the Lord" in response to receiving good news.

So the question remains, how do we bring spirituality into the workplace?

On an organizational level, one way is through the identification and deployment of corporate core values and principles (which will be covered in greater detail in Chapter 12).

The other way is more personal and brings us full circle to trusting in a higher spiritual power. The first step is to reacquaint yourself with your higher spiritual power. (I have used the term "higher spiritual power" because of its universality. But I suggest that you replace it in a way that's consistent with your own beliefs. For some it means God. For others it could be Jesus Christ and for still others, Buddha, Allah, Yahweh, etc.) Then ask yourself the following questions.

Is my conduct congruent with my beliefs?

Some people have very strong beliefs and ideas about what is right and what is wrong. It's amazing how many people do not back up what they believe with deeds. The expression "You are what you *do*" sums it up.

Am I a Jekyll and Hyde relative to my beliefs?

Some people have a split personality when it comes to living out their beliefs and values. In their personal lives, they may behave very consistently with their beliefs and values. In their professional lives, though, they seem to operate under a different set of rules. Ideally, there should be no difference. If you value honesty and demonstrate behavior consistent with that value to your children and others with whom you have a personal relationship, should it be any less important when dealing with your employees, customers, and coworkers? A great example of this was when Massachusetts-based Malden Mills burned to the ground on a cold December morning in 1995. CEO Aaron Feuerstein, a devout Jewish businessman, made a decision to rebuild the mill while continuing to pay his employees. He could have pocketed the insurance money and retired, but that would not have been consistent with his personal beliefs.

Do I spend time during the workday seeking guidance from my higher spiritual power?

A cover story in *Industry Week* talked about how a number of people in business, from CEOs to the general workforce, take time during the workday to pray, meditate, or reflect, especially when faced with challenging situations or making tough decisions. We don't have to wait for evenings or weekends to consult with our higher power! It takes only a few minutes and can be a productive way to handle difficult situations.

Do I trust in my higher spiritual power?

Don't confuse belief with trust. They're not the same thing. This point can be illustrated through the following story:

A young mountain climber, after a long, hard climb, was closing in on the summit. All of a sudden he lost his footing, slipped, and fell. In desperation he reached out, grabbed a branch, and hung on for dear life. Being relatively close to the top of the mountain, he decided to call out for help. "Is there anybody up there?" he cried out. To his relief, a voice called back, "Yes, there is. It's me, God." Being a believer, the climber was overjoyed and said, "Oh God, please help me, I can't hang on any longer!" God replied, "OK, I can help you, don't panic. You just have to do what I say." The climber shouted back, "I'll do anything, anything at all, just tell me what to do." In a clear, booming voice, God said, "*Let go of the branch.*" In exasperation and disbelief, the young man asked, "Let go of the branch?" "Yes, let go of the branch," came the reply. The climber thought for a moment, then shouted, "Is there anyone else up there?"

Trust is the seal that is placed on belief. It is the litmus test of belief. Not trusting doesn't mean we don't have belief or faith. Consider trust only a measure of belief.

How do I react to people whose beliefs are different from mine?

This is where trouble arises. There are those who think that their beliefs are the "right" beliefs. The sentiment is "Everybody else is wrong, and I am going to set them straight." We need to be mindful that people are entitled to their own beliefs. We do not have to abandon our own beliefs to be respectful and tolerant of different beliefs.

An IBM executive who attended one of my positive thinking workshops summed the "belief" trait up best during a presentation he gave. He said, "I happen to be Jewish, and these are my beliefs," which he went on to list. "But these are personal to me," he continued. "Everybody here has their own beliefs. Regardless of what you believe in, however, let me ask the following questions: Do you know what you believe in? Do you study your particular brand of religion? Do you practice it? Do you set a good example for others?" He concluded by saying, "We spend too much time worrying about what everyone believes, when we should be more concerned about our own beliefs and how we put them into practice."

BELIEF AND ITS IMPACT ON WORKPLACE PERFORMANCE

How would having belief, as we have just described it, affect your performance if you found yourself dealing with these situations?

- Being given new responsibilities that are significantly more challenging and will require you to learn new skills and/or master new technology
- Being assigned to lead a team that has a significant project goal—but a short span of time to accomplish it—while you continue to do your normal job
- Having to supervise a difficult employee—whom you cannot fire because he has "connections"
- Learning that your department will be merged with another—and, because downsizing is likely, that you will be reporting to a new boss
- Knowing that you will have to continue to work while you also take care of a seriously ill child or an elderly parent

Here is a list of application techniques that might be helpful if you want to increase your level of belief to meet these challenges or others like them.

TIPS FOR BUILDING YOUR BELIEF

1. Recognize that in order to succeed, you must have solid faith and trust in your ability to attain your goals.

This does not mean you will not sometimes fail. Making mistakes and failing are inevitable. *Believing means that your trust in your ability to succeed never wavers.*

2. Know that you already have everything you need to be successful.

If you ever doubt this, you are allowing your gifts to lie idle and will not realize your full human potential.

3. Realize that what you believe will happen has a good chance of happening.

If you are like most people, too often you think that you are not worthy or that you are incapable or lacking some necessary quality, and therefore you let yourself be held back. Know that you are worthy — and no doubt more capable than you imagine yourself to be.

4. Expect a miracle, and never allow your sense of wonder to fade.

Miracles are often the results of nonglamorous activities such as thinking, working, and persevering.

5. Never stop believing—no matter what!

The trials and tribulations of life tend to wear us down. There are times in life when things don't seem to be going our way; we stumble, fall, and sometimes stop believing in ourselves or others. Belief is the anchor that grounds us in the turbulence of life. It is life's foremost trait, overriding framework, and cornerstone. Belief is what establishes our personal set of guiding principles, forms our character, and directs our relationships. It is the beacon of light in the midst of the mist and fog. It carries you effortlessly through the storms of life, which *always* pass eventually.

CENTERING POWER: INTEGRITY

Integrity is acting on a personal commitment to honesty, openness, and fairness; living by and for one's standards.

Like belief, integrity is a centering power because it serves as an anchor that grounds us firmly before we take action, as well as during that action. It provides us with the navigational tools to guide us through the sometimes fuzzy ethical landscape of business. The word "integrity" derived from the Latin word *integer*, meaning "whole."

We demonstrate integrity each time we . . .

- Do not demonstrate conflicting or confusing points of view or attitudes toward others.
- Use consistent and appropriate criteria to measure our own behavior and performance.
- Use ethics, morals, and principles to guide our activities.
- Do not undermine or criticize others behind their backs.
- Acknowledge our own weaknesses and areas that need improvement.
- Acknowledge others' efforts and give them credit.
- Strive to create "win-win" outcomes with others.
- Do what is right even though there may be easier, more expedient solutions available.

Let's go back to the definition, because there are some important points that need to be clarified.

Integrity is *acting* on a personal commitment. It's not merely holding a moral or principled idea or position. We must act in accord with that position. Integrity is acting on a commitment to *honesty, openness, and fairness*—this, of course, is subject to our own biased interpretations of the words. Honesty includes truth, but should we tell the whole truth and nothing but the truth? Are there times when it is better to hold back the truth or parts of the truth? How open should we be with people? And what do we mean by fairness?

Let's say you are a manager who has just been told that there will be severe job cuts in your area. Among those who will be let go is an employee who, under the impression that his job was secure, recently told you that he was buying a new house.

Meanwhile, your manager has asked that you keep the news under your hat until after the holidays. You realize that your employee is about to make a major financial commitment and there's still time for him to back out of the deal. Should you tell him or keep quiet? This is just one of the many types of ethical dilemmas we face on a regular basis.

Integrity is living by and for *standards,* but whose standards? Yours? Your company's? It is the idea of standards that makes ethics in business such a slippery slope. If it means living by a company's standards, does everyone know what they are? Are they universally understood or left to individual interpretation?

> *No matter how hard you run, you can never get away from yourself. You always have you to deal with.*
>
> —DR. NORMAN VINCENT PEALE

ETHICAL DILEMMAS

Please read the following action statements. For each one, choose one of the following three statements that reflects your own sentiment about it.

A. This is terribly wrong. Anyone caught doing this should be asked to leave the company—immediately.
B. This is borderline—not terribly wrong, but something doesn't seem right either.
C. This is totally acceptable behavior. Everybody does it.

Action

1. Taking office supplies home for personal use
2. Taking office supplies home for business use
3. Searching the Web for job opportunities on company time
4. Going to the Playboy Web site during your lunch break
5. Using the phone for personal use on company time
6. Calling in sick when you're actually healthy
7. Putting a personal item in your expense report as a business expense
8. Playing golf when your boss thinks you're with a customer
9. Paying somebody off because "that's the way they do business in this country"
10. Having your secretary tell someone that you're in a meeting when you're really not

How did you respond? Was it easy for you? To explore further, ask your coworkers how they would respond. I guarantee that the responses will vary greatly. For some the choice (or decision) is a matter of interpretation. Others would say that it depends on circumstances. For those who work in companies with established policies, it's a no-brainer.

WHO SHOULD SET AND INTERPRET THE STANDARDS?

There are no easy answers to many of life's ethical dilemmas. We learn from a mixture of people: parents, teachers, clergy, friends, coworkers, and more. There was a great story by Jack Griffin in the *Chicago Sun-Times* called "It's OK, Son, Everybody Does It." It went like this:

When Johnny was six years old, he was with his father when they were caught speeding. His father handed the officer a twenty-dollar bill with his driver's license. "It's OK, son," his father said as they drove off. "Everybody does it."

When he was eight, he was present at a family council meeting presided over by Uncle George on the surest means of shaving points off the income tax return. "It's OK, kid," his uncle said. "Everybody does it."

When he was nine, his mother took him to his first theater production. The box-office man couldn't find any seats until his mother "discovered" an extra five dollars in her purse. "It's OK, son," she said. "Everybody does it."

When he was fifteen, he made right guard on the high school football team. His coach showed him how to block and at the same time grab the opposing end by the shirt so the official couldn't see it. "It's OK, kid," the coach said. "Everybody does it."

When he was sixteen, he took his first summer job at the supermarket. His assignment was to put overripe strawberries in the bottoms of boxes and the good ones on top, where they would show. "It's OK, kid," the manager said. "Everybody does it."

When he was eighteen, Johnny and a neighbor applied for a college scholarship. Johnny was a marginal student. His neighbor was in the upper 3 percent of his class, but he couldn't play right guard.

Johnny got the scholarship. "It's OK, son," his parents said. "Everybody does it."

When he was nineteen, he was approached by an upperclassman who offered him some test answers for fifty dollars. "It's OK, kid," he said. "Everybody does it."

Johnny was caught cheating and sent home in disgrace. "How could you do this to your mother and me?" his father asked. "You could never have learned anything like that at home.

"If there's one thing the adult world can't stand, it's a kid who cheats."

We learn from a number of different examples during the course of our lives. I remember when I got my first real job after finishing college. I was thrilled because it would involve business travel with an expense account. Being new to this experience, I went to my supervisor for advice on the dos and don'ts of claiming business expenses. My supervisor invited me into his office, closed the door, and said, "Scotty, my boy, let me explain to you how to play the expense game." With a wink and a nod, he proceeded to teach me every imaginable trick in the book on how to use the system to my advantage.

The key to integrity (in or out of the workplace) is to have a clearly defined set of standards that reflect your personal belief system. As you've seen in these two examples, you don't necessarily want to let other people set our standards for you.

THE PLATINUM STANDARD

In Washington, D.C., within the walls of the National Bureau of Standards, there is a one-meter length of platinum, which exists as the most perfect measure of a meter. If there is ever any doubt about the length of a meter, one can measure against the platinum standard. "Why platinum?" you may ask. Because platinum does not break down. It does not rust, corrode, expand, or shrink. It is virtually unchangeable. I recommend that each of us identify and adopt a "platinum standard" of ethics.

A "platinum standard" of ethics is something we can turn to when we are confronted with an ethical issue. For me, the "platinum standard" is based on my Christian belief system. It's different for and unique to every individual. It has served me well, especially in my professional life, where I have been faced with some tough ethical dilemmas.

I refer to my "platinum standard" especially when confronted with situations that create feelings of uneasiness and discomfort. Over time I've learned to trust these feelings, especially when my intellect says, "Don't worry about it." Sometimes all we have to go by is "feel." My friend Jim tells a great story about trusting your "gut feel." A few years ago, he was a young advertising executive who had just taken a job with the Polaroid Company, famous for the Polaroid Land Camera. He reported directly to its founder, Edwin Land, who had invented the technology. One day Jim met with Dr. Land because he was responsible for all advertising, which included television, and he wanted to be sure that he produced commercials that were in good taste. In a sense, he wanted to know what Dr. Land's policy was on television advertising. So he asked him, "Dr. Land, how will I know if my commercials are in good taste?" Dr. Land responded by saying, "Imagine many years from now you're sitting in your living room watching television with your five-year-old grandson on your knee. All of a sudden one of your commercials is replayed, and your grandson looks up into your eyes and asks, 'Grandpa, was that one of your commercials?' Well, Jim, if you can look him in the eye with pride and say, 'Yeah, that was one of mine,' you know you've done all right." Jim went on to manage the production of some of the most successful, tasteful commercials ever seen on television, among them the wildly successful ones featuring Mariette Hartley and James Garner.

TIPS FOR BUILDING YOUR INTEGRITY

1. Question your motives; apply your situation against the ethical checklist.
In Dr. Peale's and Ken Blanchard's book *The Power of Ethical Management*, they outline a three-point litmus test for dealing with ethical issues:
Always ask yourself:
- Is it legal and in line with organizational policy? If what you are doing or about to do is illegal or against organizational policy, your decision should be simple — don't do it!

- Is it fair to all concerned in both the short and long term? If it's somehow exclusionary or has benefits over the long haul for only certain people, don't do it!
- In the end, how will I feel about myself? Would I like it if my actions were broadcast for all to hear?

The last is the most important of the three, because there are many things that might be legal or in line with organizational policy but might still be wrong ethically. For example, at one time slavery was legal in this country. Did that make it right? Doing business in China is perfectly legal, but for some it raises an important moral issue. A few years ago, as trade with that country began to open up, Bob Haas of Levi Strauss decided that because of the government's human rights violations, he would not do business there. Other CEOs derided him for making such a foolhardy decision. They didn't understand why he would turn his back on all the potential money to be made.

2. Practice what you preach.
Does your character match your actions? Do not ask others to do anything that you yourself would not do. Know what you really believe in.

> We lie loudest when we lie to ourselves.
> —ERIC HOFFER

3. Be your own investigative reporter.
Once a week, imagine yourself an investigative reporter accompanying you to work, on business trips, around your home, and elsewhere. Imagine the reporter listening in on your phone conversations, sharing your mail, and observing your actions. What kind of story do you think the reporter would write? Would you be proud of it? What, if anything, would you change?

4. Keep your commitments.
When you say you will do something, do your associates believe you really will, or do they have some doubt? Promises should not be made lightly unless we want them to be taken lightly.

5. Learn to say "no."

Develop the ability to say "no" to things for which you have no time, talent, or sincere interest. By learning to say "no" to such things, you will be able to say "yes" to the ones that matter most. Don't try to be all things to all people; you'll end up disappointing a great many of them.

6. Build and maintain your integrity.

The two most sought after qualities of a top executive are honesty and loyalty. Spend a moment or two reflecting on why those are the top two.

CENTERING POWER: FOCUS

Focus is the directed attention through the setting of goals and priorities.

You've no doubt heard the saying "If you don't know where you're going, you could end up anywhere." Focus is a centering power because it arises from a place deep within each of us. It is derived from the Latin word "focus," meaning hearth, or place where rays of heat come together. Knowing what you want out of life is crucial if you want to make something of yourself. Too many of us cruise around like unguided missiles, hoping to strike some unknown or ill-defined target.

We demonstrate focus each time we . . .

- Have a clear vision of what we want to accomplish in life.
- Do not let others or current situations discourage us or interfere with our vision.
- Take time to plan and prioritize our activities.
- Think about the benefits of achieving our goals.
- Concentrate our energy on activities that will help us achieve our goals.
- Undertake efforts that support our personal and professional development.

When your thoughts are in confusion, you live in an unreal world, and you cannot see your way up and out of it.
—DR. NORMAN VINCENT PEALE

In Chapter 5 I discussed goal setting in the context of specific business situations. In this segment we're going to consider the concept of focus to include goal setting, but from an overall view.

SCOTT ADAMS, CREATOR OF THE "DILBERT" COMIC STRIP

As a child, Scott Adams always wanted to be a cartoonist, but he decided to major in economics in college after earning a low grade in a drawing course. Armed with his degree, he became a middle manager at Pacific Bell in northern California, making about $70,000 a year. However, after seventeen years with the company, he felt fed up and very disappointed that he rarely dealt directly with customers, which he valued doing more than his supervisory responsibilities. With mounting dissatisfaction, he decided to refocus his career. He began by writing down his goals and then began practicing a simple affirmation, which he wrote *fifteen* times a day. By putting his vision into the words "I will become a syndicated cartoonist," he took the first major step toward focusing on his ultimate career dream. Adams later explained to a reporter that once he regularly reaffirmed his goals, he began to notice things happening that made his goals more likely to become reality. He sent out many packages with his cartoons to the various syndication services. After receiving numerous rejections, United Media, the home of his idol, Charles Schulz, decided to syndicate his cartoon.

After receiving his syndication contract, Adams worked harder than ever at "Dilbert," but a year later only a hundred newspapers were carrying it. Frustrated, he created a new goal: to discover why the cartoon strip wasn't selling better. He began gathering feedback from his customers and learned that business-oriented comic strips were being cut out and hung on walls all over corporate America. So he refocused his cartoon themes to 80 percent business and technology issues. And the rest is history! His best-selling books have sold millions of copies. So what is Scott Adams focused on these days? His new affirmation is "I will win the Pulitzer Prize."

THE RELATIONSHIP BETWEEN BELIEF AND FOCUS

Scott Adams's dream was to be a syndicated cartoonist. A dream or vision is nothing more than an image in the mind. One of the greatest dreamers ever was Walt Disney. Disney was determined to bring the magic of fantasy directly to his audience. According to a story on Disney appearing in *Forbes Greatest Business Stories of All Time* by Daniel Gross, he wanted a way to truly bring his vision to life. After watching his two daughters play on a merry-go-round, he conceived of the idea of a theme park: "I felt there should be something built, some kind of a family park, where parents and children could have fun together." Unable to secure approval from his studio, which was controlled in part by several important stockholders, he started another company, Walt Disney, Inc., launching it with his own money. His ability to "see the unseeable" made it difficult at times to find backers who were able to see what he saw, but he never stopped focusing on his dream.

There aren't enough people in business today who dream about the endless possibilities for themselves or for their companies. It all starts with belief: understanding who we are, what we stand for, and what we're capable of.

Armed with this understanding, we can seek out our purpose and begin to focus on it. Focus is like a laser beam: it draws all our innate powers together with unswerving commitment to bring our ideas into reality.

The greatest thing in this world is not so much where we are, but in what direction we are moving.

— OLIVER WENDELL HOLMES

TIPS FOR BUILDING YOUR FOCUS

1. Know what you want.

This may seem elementary, but it is in fact the most important step. There are two levels of "knowing." On the macro level, it's having a clear vision of what you want to accomplish in *life*. This is *big*. Do you have a clear vision of what you want? Are you where you want to be right now relative to your vision? On the micro level, it's having a clear vision of what you want out of specific types of activities. Martin Luther King had a vision that someday all races would be treated equally. He focused all of his attention on making that a reality. At the macro level, it was what he wanted to accomplish in his life. On a day-to-day basis, he focused his attention on specific activities (delivering speeches, organizing marches, practicing civil disobedience, and so on) in order to accomplish smaller goals that would promote his larger one. We may not feel as though our vision is on a par with Martin Luther King's. We may even struggle with the idea of having a "grand vision" for life. But each of us can dream big dreams and direct our attention to their fulfillment.

Having clear individual goals and linking them to team and company goals goes a long way toward providing purpose and direction. Here are some examples that I've come across in my travels:

"Achieve the highest customer satisfaction rating in my division."
"Become the first woman to become CEO of my company."
"Provide timely, open, honest feedback to my department."
"Help my staff realize their potential within the company."

According to a study conducted by the Conference Board, goals serve a number of key functions. They:

- Direct one's attention and action to the tasks needing completion.
- Mobilize one's energy and effort, intensifying them where necessary.
- Provide a performance evaluation mechanism that will help increase one's persistence when progress or improvement is slow.
- Motivate one to seek out strategies for achieving results.
- Clarify one's expectations.
- Increase one's intrinsic motivation to achieve.
- Enhance one's pride, self-satisfaction, and self-confidence.

Once you see what you are after in the "theater of the mind," you will need to (a) set concrete SMART goals, (b) write down and practice saying your affirmations, and (c) visualize the outcomes you desire. (You may wish to review Chapter 5 on goal setting.)

Image your goal. Hold that image in consciousness. Keep that image always before you, and your goal will materialize.
— DR. NORMAN VINCENT PEALE

2. Clear your mind and desk of all other projects and issues so you can focus exclusively on the task at hand.

In other words, eliminate all possible distractions. Become a "mono-maniac" and focus exclusively on the task or activity with which you are engaged. I know this is difficult, because my desk, even if it is clear when I arrive at work in the morning, quickly becomes cluttered with the business of the day. It takes discipline to break what I have found to be nothing more than a poor work habit, but it is possible. By doing so, you'll reach your goal faster and better than if you allow yourself to be distracted by phone calls, concerns about other important projects, worries about whether you'll succeed, and other such matters. Professional athletes and highly successful business professionals plan, prepare, and execute, *staying in the moment* (or "zone"), and *avoid worrying* about how things will turn out. The most important thing is to empty your mind of all the nonessentials: worry, concerns, other trivial projects, and so on.

In one of Dr. Peale's books I read about an imagery technique on how to remove clutter from our minds. Over the years, it has worked well for me. The idea is to "empty your mind" in the same way you empty your pockets before retiring at night. Imagine reaching into your mind and pulling out all the unnecessary junk in there. Take everything out that is unrelated to the task at hand. You can throw it all away if you like. Or if you prefer, you can put it all back when you're finished with your task. Close your eyes and actually *see* all the clutter being removed. This "mental Drano" treatment works wonders. Being focused *on one thing at a time* is critical to achieving your goals, hopes, and dreams.

Never worry until it's time *to worry.*

3. Don't allow others to discourage or dissuade you from achieving your vision.

We often look to others for approval of our dreams and vision of the future. We hear things like "Oh, that'll never work" or "What a crazy idea." When faced with opposition, we allow others to dissuade us. Years ago, an inventor I know developed a prototype for what promised to be an exciting new consumer product. His idea was met with pessimism from friends and family alike.

Eventually he abandoned the idea. About three years later, an identical product was introduced into the market—by someone else—and was met with incredible success.

4. Focus, but do not lose sight of the big picture.

Some matters are worth only so much time and effort. Avoid turning your present challenge into a "win at all costs" situation if other *important* matters will suffer. Choose your battles wisely, and you will win the war. We live in an interdependent world. Sometimes we selfishly pursue our dreams at the expense of others. We close our eyes and sometimes fail to see that our pursuits have caused other issues to arise.

Our centering power comes from a place deep within ourselves and prepares us to meet the challenges, both known and unknown, that lie ahead. Tapping into this magnificent power enables us to meet challenges with a steady, unwavering conviction.

8

Uplifting Power

Uplifting Power is the power to energize ourselves in mind, body, and spirit as we move on to great things. It is a form of self-motivation for when we have to do something we don't particularly want to or the road gets bumpy and uncertain. Sometimes we need Uplifting Power to get us moving; other times we need to tap into it along the journey, when we feel as if we are stuck in a rut.

UPLIFTING POWER: OPTIMISM

Optimism is a belief in and expectation of positive outcomes, even in the face of difficulty, challenge, or crisis.

Optimism is often confused with positive thinking. People use the terms interchangeably, but, as we learned in Chapter 2, they're not the same; *all* positive thinkers are optimistic, but not all optimists are positive thinkers! The word "optimism" derives from the Latin word *optimus*, meaning "best."

We demonstrate optimism each time we . . .

- See the benefits of and positive opportunities in a crisis, problem, or difficulty.
- Assume or expect success, satisfaction, or achievement in an endeavor.
- Identify the limitless possibilities we have to shape the life we desire.

- Meet a challenge or address a new opportunity with a feeling of control.
- Eliminate or diminish the impact of fears, doubts, and concerns, whether internal or external.
- Keep our spirit up despite difficult circumstances.
- Tackle problems with a mind-set of "how," not "if," they can be solved.

Maintaining a hopeful, expectant attitude during challenging times is critical in the work environment. It can make all the difference between successful outcomes and unsuccessful ones. Pessimism, meanwhile, is a pervasive expectation of negative outcomes.

Pessimism nevertheless has some redeeming points. I remember having a discussion with a business acquaintance who commented, "I'm not a pessimist, just a realist." The fact is that pessimism can be reality-based. And there's nothing wrong with being grounded in reality. According to Dr. Martin Seligman, professor of psychology at the University of Pennsylvania, depressed people, many of whom are also pessimists, accurately judge how much control they have over various situations. Optimists, on the other hand, believe they have much more control over situations than they really do—even when they are helpless and have no control at all! The pessimist sees the stark reality of situations, which to some degree can be useful in the business setting.

Think of those who have financial responsibility in an organization. These people deal with facts and figures every day. The good news is that we can count on them to be the voices of reason when making major financially based decisions. There is such a thing as healthy pessimism in business—it causes us to proceed with caution and encourages us to be more careful, thoughtful, wise, and analytical. But too often, pessimism gets in the way of creative brainstorming, idea generation, and problem solving. The pessimists justify their role by suggesting that they are looking after the good of the organization. Although that's true to an extent, I have found that pessimists in business are often pervasively pessimistic, meaning that the pessimism extends to all aspects of their jobs. And more than likely, they're also pessimistic outside their jobs. The point is that *some* pessimism in the workplace can be healthy in certain situations, but too much can be damaging.

As I am optimistic myself, there have been times in my career when I consciously sought out a pessimist for advice on an important matter. Also, when forming project teams I generally make sure that I have at least one pessimist on the team. Although they have to be well managed to avoid bringing down the morale of those around them, I have found them extremely helpful. Since I tend to be very optimistic, I sometimes "run without looking." Having a pessimist close by never diminishes my optimism. What it does do is help me slow down and consider all the possible ramifications of my decisions. There have been times when I have hesitated to seek the pessimist's counsel because I did not want to hear what would be said. But I realized that as long as I kept everything in perspective, I would be OK.

This habit has stayed with me over the years, and I have found it to be the best method of keeping my sometimes out-of-control optimism in check!

Like the successful company, we each have in us an executive who balances the counsels of daring against the counsels of doom. By understanding the single virtue of pessimism, along with its pervasive crippling consequences, we can learn to resist pessimism's constant callings, as deep-seated in brain or in habit as they may be. We can learn to choose optimism for the most part, but also to heed pessimism when it is warranted.
—MARTIN SELIGMAN, NOTED PSYCHOLOGIST

Overall, pervasive pessimism is not a good thing. Studies show that pessimism lowers the immune system, slowing down the body's natural healing process. It promotes depression and passivity when dealing with setbacks. It contributes to anxiety and poor physical health. Pessimists also tend to mentally allow setbacks to snowball into disasters and then into catastrophes, thereby creating a self-fulfilling prophecy: "Everything is as bad as or worse than I thought."

Optimism, on the other hand, raises the immune system, helps us bounce back more quickly from setbacks, and keeps us from giving up, especially when confronted with obstacles. According to Michael F. Scheier, Ph.D., professor of psychology at Carnegie Mellon University in Pittsburgh, pessimists view setbacks as signs that things will never be the same. But to an optimist they are simply something to overcome. When something goes wrong, optimists tend to blame it on external, temporary forces within their control; pessimists, though, blame trouble on their own innate character or personality. A pessimist who gets a lousy performance review might say, "I'm so incompetent. I'll never amount to anything," whereas an optimist will say, "My performance was not up to par. I'll need to knuckle down and try harder this quarter." Optimists usually *expect* the best outcome, so they're generally more motivated to bring it into reality.

THE POWER OF OPTIMISM

In November 1999, I ran the New York City Marathon. Out of approximately 31,000 entrants, I finished around 11,000th, at just over four hours. It was slightly slower than my previous year's time of three hours, fifty-eight minutes, but I was pretty happy with the results. Still feeling euphoric about my accomplishment a few days later, I picked up a copy of *The New York Times* that happened to have a feature story about another runner in the marathon: Zoe Koplowitz. Many of you who follow the sport may never have heard of Zoe Koplowitz. That's because we usually hear only about the top finishers. Zoe is famous not for being the first to finish but for coming in *last*. In fact, Zoe's official time was *thirty* hours, fifty minutes, fifteen seconds. Running a marathon requires a high level of optimism, especially when you're deep into the race. Your legs feel like lead. You're tired and ache all over, and all you want to do is lie down and go to sleep. What makes Zoe so remarkable is that in addition to the strain of a marathon, she has multiple sclerosis and is diabetic, and shortly before the race she fell and cracked a rib and separated her shoulder. Yet despite all these setbacks, she ran relentlessly through the five boroughs of New York City and throughout the night, escorted by the Guardian Angels for protection. What an incredible living, breathing testimony to the power of the human spirit and optimism. According to the *Times* story, Zoe says, "I feel like a human Post-it note—I remind people anything is possible." She then goes on to say, "This is my opportunity to get my personal agenda in. To show people I don't have anything that they don't have. I don't wear a supercape; I don't go into a phone booth and change into a superhero to do a marathon. I am who you are and that's the whole point."

We rejoice in our sufferings, because we know that suffering produces perseverance; perseverance, character; character, hope. And hope does not disappoint us.
—ROMANS, 5:3–5

Now go back and review the definition of optimism. What word or words stand out? Most people think that optimism is something you feel when things are going your way:

- Your boss tells you unofficially that the promotion you've been waiting for is going to happen by the end of the year.
- A customer practically guarantees you that an order is yours.
- According to those in the know, the funding for your project will be approved by week's end.

When you think a positive outcome is virtually certain, it's easy to be optimistic. The wind is blowing at your back, and the future looks bright and hopeful. But what happens when the wind begins to shift? The promotion you've been expecting is put on hold due to a just-announced pending merger; your customer announces spending cutbacks; consensus on the funding for your project was not reached . . .

The true test of optimism is whether or not you remain hopeful of a positive outcome even when the indicators suggest otherwise. What happens to your optimism when it is faced with the first obstacle? Where is it when the roadblocks, problems, and challenges continue to heap up?

What if your boss comes to you and says, "Hey, Jack, about that transfer we discussed recently, I have some bad news, and I have some worse news. Which do you want first?" Where do you think your level of optimism would be at that point?

SITUATIONAL OPTIMISM: WHAT TRIGGERS *YOUR* OPTIMISM?

There are few people who never feel optimistic. In general, most of us are *sporadic* pessimists. Depending on the situation we are involved in and the facts that are presenting themselves at the time, we find that our level of optimism shifts. As problems appear and show no sign of letting up, our hopeful, optimistic thoughts, feelings, and behaviors become more pessimistic. To discover your turning point or trigger, read through the following situations and decide which two or three in each category tend to make you think, feel, and act less optimistically.

Being Managed

1. A new supervisor who doesn't know or appreciate my value
2. Receiving (or not receiving) performance reviews or feedback
3. Changing priorities or unrealistic deadlines from management
4. Lack of clear direction or expectations by management
5. Missing out on a promotion or new job assignment
6. Being left out of decisions or plans
7. Not being recognized or rewarded for performance
8. Differences in personal and/or managerial styles
9. Feeling bored or underdeveloped in my position
10. Lack of communication with my manager on work progress, issues, or opportunities

Managing Others

11. Giving performance reviews or feedback to others
12. Having to deal with conflicts among others
13. Too many demands from others for my time and attention
14. Employees who do not take initiative, make decisions, or act empowered
15. Lack of resources (quality and/or quantity) to get a job done
16. Dealing with style differences among employees
17. Being kept "out of the loop" on important issues, problems, or decisions
18. Not being told the whole truth, especially regarding problems or issues

19. Having to deal with personal problems
20. Treating everyone fairly but not always the same

Organization and Culture
21. Company politics and game playing
22. "Shooting the messenger" who delivers bad news
23. Policies, processes, or systems that hinder progress, new ideas, or exceptions to the norm
24. Reorganization, reengineering, downsizing, and so on
25. Constant forced changes in direction, focus, and areas of responsibility
26. Lack of career growth/opportunities to develop
27. Bureaucratic structures, reporting relationships, layers
28. Merging with other companies, new alliances, new products or services
29. Insufficient communication and dialogue about what is happening and why

Peer and Customer Relationships
30. Company gossip or the "grapevine"
31. Opinions or feedback on my performance that goes to others, not me
32. Feeling or knowing that I am being lied to, blamed, or patronized
33. Not being able to negotiate over projects, deadlines, requests
34. Being left out of decisions or problem solving that affects me and/or my employees

Other Situations
35. If other relevant situations occur to you, identify and list them on a separate piece of paper.

Now go back and review your responses. Was there any particular category or categories that had an inordinate number of check marks? If so, it may be an area you will want to investigate further. For instance, you may have discovered that the area that lowers your optimism the most is in the area of "organization and culture." In this case, it is very possible that when things are seemingly completely out of your control, you take a more pessimistic posture. People in high places are making the decisions for you, and you feel there is little you can do to affect the outcome. In this case you have at least three choices. You can accept the situation as it is, try to change or impact the situation, or, as a last resort, remove yourself from it.

If "managing others" received several check marks, it's possible that it's a result of your managing style. You may feel you lack certain skills, education, or experience to manage effectively. It's also possible that you lack confidence when managing certain people in certain situations. Any explanation is possible, but what's most important is that regardless of the explanation, you can increase your level of optimism in *any* situation.

Pinpointing Your Threshold of Optimism

The first step in increasing your level of optimism is to try to determine the point at which it shifts to pessimism. I'll use a sports example as an illustration. At the start of the NFL season in 1999, one team, the New York Jets, had been pegged by many sports analysts and commentators as a serious contender for making it to the Super Bowl. Bolstered by the success of the previous season, the current roster, and the coaching talent, the team's level of optimism was off the charts. Then, the first Sunday of the new season, the team's star quarterback, Vinny Testaverde, took a snap, dropped back to pass, and crumbled to the ground in excruciating pain. The cause was a ruptured Achilles tendon. It ended the season for Testaverde. In the blink of an eye, the level of optimism, which had been so high, shifted to a very high level of pessimism—so high that in effect it ended the season for the team as well. I watched that situation closely. The team lost the next several games. The loss of Testaverde was too much for it to overcome. Later in the season, under a backup quarterback, it started racking up some wins—though by then it was too late to bounce back completely to make the playoffs. The team members' biggest problem had been to allow their pessimism to get the best of them.

The event that caused the shift in this case was specific and acute. The team had based its optimism on the hope that its quarterback would remain healthy for the season. In fact, it based its entire season on that hope. Optimism needs to be based on a belief that extends beyond any one individual. It should include a belief in one's own capabilities, as well as others' — in this case the team's and coaching staff's capabilities.

This lesson applies equally in the workplace. It is wise to ask ourselves, "Why am I so optimistic about this situation?" and then list the reasons. Make sure you're basing your high level of optimism on more than one factor. If not, one single, acute event may quickly cause your optimism to shift to a stifling level of pessimism. If you're the type of person whose optimism shifts quickly to pessimism once an obstacle pops up, it may be helpful to examine your level of belief, courage, and confidence. There's a strong relationship among them, and there is a way to leverage them to avoid the shift from optimism to pessimism. By doing so, we can develop a capability to maintain our optimism for longer periods before giving up all hope. Optimism is based on hope, and hope is based on belief. We also need the fortitude to withstand occasional — often temporary — setbacks. Another effective method of boosting and/or maintaining our optimism is to reorient how we view certain obstacles and setbacks. We can do this by applying the truth-in-thinking technique discussed in Chapter 4.

The tough-minded optimist views any problem as a challenge to his intelligence, ingenuity, and faith. . . . He knows there is a solution, and so he finally finds it.
—DR. NORMAN VINCENT PEALE

It has taken me years to gain control over my own optimism-to-pessimism shifts. I have reoriented my thinking to view challenges, problems, and setbacks differently. It has become clear to me that setbacks are inevitable — a part of life. I have also come to the realization that setbacks are part of what makes me grow, especially when I view them in a positive manner. Setbacks now embolden and invigorate me. They challenge me, sometimes tauntingly, and dare me to overcome them.

Rising to the occasion is sometimes painful. It's easier to give in and give up. But in the long run, I have found that it pays to maintain my optimism and meet the setbacks head-on. I am reminded of these words from Nietzsche: "That which does not kill me makes me stronger."

Don't wait for the right time to be optimistic. Many people adopt the mind-set that once a given obstacle is removed, they will be able to be optimistic:

"Once I get my new promotion . . ."
"Once I get my life in order . . ."
"Once I pay off all my loans . . ."
"Once I find the right person . . ."
"Once my boss retires . . ."

Life's too short to wait for the perfect set of circumstances to be optimistic.

Tips for Building Your Optimism

1. Write a positive affirmation to overcome a specific obstacle.
Acknowledge and accept the fact that you possess all the strength you'll ever need to handle anything you will have to face.

2. Conduct a realistic assessment of the situation.
Especially when faced with an increasingly tough situation, assess it objectively for what it truly is. No doubt it has its negative aspects, which should not be denied. But similarly, *every* negative situation has opportunity within it.

3. For whatever challenge you may be facing, relax and think of as many viable options as you can.
If appropriate, enlist the help of others. As you identify possible solutions and implement them, your level of optimism is sure to rise.

4. Remember: Life is an ongoing cycle of ups and downs.
Think back to other times you have faced similar situations and emerged victorious. Don't allow yourself to ride an emotional roller coaster. Bad situations can quickly change into good situations and vice versa. It's important to find a balance and evenness in our emotions.

5. Don't be afraid to be optimistic.

I've found that one of the biggest reasons for people not being more optimistic is that they don't want to be disappointed. Some people rationalize that if they don't have high expectations, they won't be let down when the expectations don't materialize: "I didn't expect to get the job anyway, so I'm okay." This is a sad state of affairs. A person in this position is a person who won't allow himself to hope for great things. And without hope, there's little we can ever accomplish.

The last point I'd like to make about optimism is that it is possible to overdo it. Some people stubbornly refuse to let go of hope, even when it becomes clear that all hope is gone. This may sound like a contradiction to the notion of hope, which is the cornerstone of optimism. The time to abandon an idea, a dream, or any kind of a quest is not always obvious. It requires a certain amount of discernment and introspection to know whether to let go or not. If we miss the signal telling us when to let go, we risk missing out on other opportunities. (I'll explore the concept of "letting go" in more depth in Chapter 9, where I'll discuss one of the Driving Powers: determination.)

UPLIFTING POWER: ENTHUSIASM

Enthusiasm is having high levels of interest, positive energy, passion, and personal motivation.

Enthusiasm is the second of our uplifting powers. Enthusiasm is the spark that gets us and others mobilized and spiritually ready to dive into our projects, interests, goals, and dreams. It is the source of energy that motivates us from a deep place within us when we feel stalled or stuck. The word "enthusiasm" derives from the Greek word *entheos*, meaning "inspired." It literally means "possessed by a god" or *en theos*, "in God."

We demonstrate enthusiasm each time we . . .

- Seize opportunities to make things happen.
- Wake up feeling excited about the day ahead.
- Show a noticeably high energy and activity level relative to others'.
- Look forward to and welcome new experiences and challenges.
- Volunteer our efforts without being asked.
- Overtly communicate our convictions.

- Thrive on discovering our dreams, interests, desires, and passions.
- Show a contagious energy or fervor about projects, ideas, and opportunities.

What goes on in the mind is what determines the outcome.
When an individual really gets enthusiasm, you can see it in the
flash of the eyes, in the alert and vibrant personality. You can
see it in the verve of the whole being. Enthusiasm makes the
difference in one's attitude toward other people, toward one's
job, toward the world. It makes the big difference in the zest
and delight of human existence.
— Dr. Norman Vincent Peale

We tend to think that the only people in business who need high levels of enthusiasm are salespeople, customer service people, people in any function in business that requires frequent direct contact with customers. It is a big mistake, though, to limit our thinking on enthusiasm like that. Just a few months ago I was conducting a coaching session for a midlevel manager of a large technology company. We were reviewing his positive thinking inventory results, which overall showed a nice balance in how he manages the ten traits on a day-to-day basis. His one concern, though, was that the inventory indicated that he generally runs low on enthusiasm. As a manager of an internal support function, he had little, if any, contact with external customers. He was concerned because he *did* have frequent contact with his internal customers—the staff. He cited many examples when he had felt he was unable to inspire and motivate his staff, especially when presenting new ideas or plans. He felt his lack of enthusiasm sent the wrong message, and he was right. Transmitting ideas, plans, and projects in a dull, mundane way does little to enlist the support of others. I probed deeper with this manager because I wanted to be clear about the source of his low enthusiasm. I thought it might have been a result of a lack of interest or burnout—he was a twenty-year veteran of the company.

As it turned out, he loved his job, his company, and the people he worked with. It had more to do with his *expression* of enthusiasm. He was by nature a low-key, thoughtful, methodical individual. He said he didn't have it in him to have the exuberant animation of some of his peers. We eventually turned the discussion to how he could exude enthusiasm without being insincere or phony. He agreed that others' perception of his low enthusiasm was hurting him professionally. He felt it was holding him back in his career. For in this particular company, a premium was placed on charismatic, high-energy people, especially if they hoped to aspire to higher levels within the company. We ultimately came up with a specific plan as to how he could crank up his enthusiasm, especially when interacting with staff and senior management.

Mary Kay Ash, founder of Mary Kay Cosmetics, has this to say about enthusiasm: "A good manager arouses enthusiasm. Many talented individuals fail for lack of enthusiasm . . . for this reason managers must be able to arouse enthusiasm in their people. And in order to accomplish this, they themselves must first be enthusiastic. Of course nobody can be up all the time, and contrary to what many people think of me, I'm not always up either. I just don't let anybody know when I'm not!"

Having low or no enthusiasm is very different from not exuding enthusiasm. If you feel you lack sufficient enthusiasm, there is a way to remedy that lack.

WHAT TRIGGERS YOUR ENTHUSIASM?

Make a list of five things you love to do, things that interest, energize, and motivate you. They may include hobbies, interests, sports, or work-related activities. Take a few minutes now to prepare your list on a sheet of paper.

The next step is to select a couple of them that are the most motivating to you.

Recall a *specific* occasion or event when you were doing each of these activities. Think about where you were, whom you were with, what you were doing, and how you expressed your interest, energy, and enthusiasm. Write a brief description of the occasion or event on your list. Make a column and note the motivators of each of the things you love to do the most.

Now review your list and identify the critical ingredients.

What Made This Activity Especially Stimulating and Enjoyable?

Was it . . .

- The intellectual challenge?
- The involvement of others?
- Learning something new?
- The freedom to do what you want?
- Accomplishing something worthwhile?
- Experimentation and discovery?
- Being creative or innovative?
- Producing something others will enjoy and/or use?
- The outdoors or nature?
- Travel or adventure?
- Planning and organizing?
- Influencing or helping others?
- Working or playing alone?
- Having a peaceful, relaxing time?
- Competing against others or a standard?
- Spontaneous activity?
- Meeting a personal goal?
- Discussions or conversations with others?
- Nonstructured activities?
- Physical challenges or activities?
- Working with your hands?
- Fantasy, drama, imagineering?
- Appreciating something beautiful, creative, or interesting?
- Other (list)

Can you identify trends, patterns, or similar characteristics among your favorite things to do? Which aspects seem to create the most energy and motivation in you? Identifying your triggers of enthusiasm will help you seek out opportunities that are congruent with them.

The Power of Enthusiasm in Business

Recall a time when you felt tremendous enthusiasm or were very energized in your job. Think about the event or occasion. What was the focus? What were the key elements? I remember that when I was in college there was a geology professor named Dr. Groff. He was one of the most enthusiastic, cheerful people I had ever met. Dr. Groff would walk down the hallway with a long, purposeful stride, arms swinging. He'd have a smile on his face that seemed to indicate that there was some incredible secret behind it. One day as he passed by me, a friend with whom I had been chatting noticed him and the energy emanating from him. She said, "Scott, when I get out of college, I want to find a job that would make me feel the way Dr. Groff seems to feel. He's always smiling, he seems so happy. He really seems to enjoy what he does." Neither of us could imagine how this guy could get so excited about rocks! The next semester I decided to sign up for his class on National Parks and Monuments. I was a marketing major, but I took the class as an elective because I wanted to see what made the guy tick! As I got to know him, it became obvious. He simply *loved* what he did. He loved every aspect of it: the subject matter itself, teaching, interacting with students, learning, everything. His voice was filled with enthusiasm. He made rocks and rock formations interesting, fun, and enjoyable. Was he somehow immune to the politics and bureaucracy of the university? Of course not. He had to deal with them just like everyone else.

But he loved what he did so much that he was able to put the annoying aspects aside. He dealt with the challenges without letting them get the best of him.

Sometimes when we feel that our enthusiasm for our job is at an all-time low, we need to recall and try to resurrect the passion we once felt for it. Losing (or diminishing) passion happens in relationships all the time. And in many ways, your career is like a relationship. It's tempting to abandon the relationship for the excitement of something new. But before doing so, it's worth trying to rekindle the flame.

I was recently talking with a manager in a company that is known for putting people on a fast track, moving them up in the ranks. But the company moves slowly with some people. The manager was unhappy because even as a bright, good worker she couldn't seem to get where she wanted to go as fast as she wanted to. "I think I've got to start looking for opportunities outside the company," she said. "I'm too frustrated and no longer enjoy coming to work. I think I want to get into social work, where I feel I can make a useful contribution helping people." I cautioned her that even though it was possible that it might be the time for her to move on, she shouldn't make any rash decisions. I suggested that she continue to focus on her work, doing the best job she knew how to. Then I suggested that she try volunteering her time on evenings and weekends in agencies that focused on social needs that matched her interests to see if she really thought she could do that kind of work full-time. Finally, I suggested that she talk over some of her issues with her manager to see if there were other opportunities within her department that she could be involved in—something that would provide a challenge and thus boost her enthusiasm.

She agreed, and three months later, when I called her as part of a follow-up, I thought I was talking to a different person. She told me that she had begun doing volunteer work with a local agency. And although she enjoyed the work, she did not feel that she was ready to jump in full-time at that point in her life. Next she said that her manager had given her a new assignment representing about 20 percent of her daily workload. She said that the project was right up her alley and she was so involved with it that she had postponed her job-seeking activities.

I believe that two things occurred with her. First, she felt stuck and thought she could find something better elsewhere. Second, she had moved too far away from the tasks that had originally brought her pleasure. In the end, her experimentation with the volunteer work made her appreciate her job much more. And by taking on a new project, she rediscovered an underlying, perhaps latent motivator.

Let's go back to the list you made earlier. Which current work-related activities and projects make you feel the most enthusiastic, passionate, and energized? Have you found their common denominator(s)? For instance, if the event you recalled was the public presentation of a new product, which you found highly enjoyable because it involved considerable risk, think about seeking out projects or responsibilities that incorporate similar uncertainty and speculation.

Next, consider the current work-related activities and projects that you *do not* feel enthusiastic about. For each, ask yourself whether there is any way you can build in or increase any of the critical enthusiasm-building ingredients that you've already identified. If your answer is "yes," what action can you take to inject more enthusiasm into at least one work-related activity or project listed?

If your answer is "no," you might try to identify other outlets at work, such as volunteering for your organization's chosen charity, serving as an internal committee member, or participating on an employee sports team.

You might also consider engaging in similar activities outside the workplace. Sometimes our lack of enthusiasm on the job actually has more to do with our dissatisfaction with other aspects of our lives—a personal relationship, home life, personal problems, and so forth.

> *If there's no fun in it, something is wrong with all you're doing.*
> —Dr. Norman Vincent Peale

As discussed earlier, having enthusiasm means being inspired. Inspiration fuels passion. If you don't have passion for what you do, you won't have enthusiasm for it. Passion comes from attaching significance to what we do. It comes from finding meaning and purpose in what we do, even if it's not glamorous. A few years ago, when I was on a business trip to Atlanta, my host treated me to breakfast at a popular breakfast place. The place was packed with businesspeople—who aren't always the most patient customers! Our waitress was working terribly hard, rushing back and forth ʳing orders, delivering food, cleaning tables, handling mᵒ ˡing with complaints. But the entire time we ˟ her lose her composure. Instead, she smiled ᵗ this, my inquisitive host asked, "How do you ᵈ e to stay so pleasant in the midst of all this chᵃ 'Wait a minute, I'll be right back, and then I'll later she came back to the table with her orᵈ pad to reveal the cardboard backing. Taped were pictures of her young children. "These are ᵗ ᵖᵣₑₒᵢₒᵤₛ people in my life," she said. "I'm a single mom. Theyᵈₑpend on me to take care of them and provide a good living. If I don't do a good job, if I don't take good care of my customers, then I can't take care of my children, and they're counting on me every day. That's how I do it." I'll never forget that woman. She made a powerful impression on me and my host. She had found meaning and purpose in what she did.

During a recent conference in New York City, Bill Pollard, chairman and CEO of ServiceMaster, told of a conversation he had struck up with one of his employees whose job was primarily to mop floors. Bill was visiting one of the company's clients, a hospital, and noticed her mopping up the floors with great enthusiasm. "How is it that you find so much joy in what you do?" he asked her. She replied, "Mr. Pollard, by keeping the floors clean, I am creating a clean, safe environment that helps the nurses and doctors do their jobs, which is to make people healthy." She connected her job with making people healthy. She had discovered the purpose of what she did, and it motivated her beyond measure.

When you're enthusiastic, you have high levels of interest, passion, positive energy, and personal motivation. By identifying the critical ingredients in your favorite activities, you can seek work-related opportunities that also spark your natural enthusiasm. When confronted with a project or job responsibilities that drain your enthusiasm, investigate whether there are *any* critical enthusiasm-building ingredients present.

Enthusiasm sells. Others are more likely to listen to you if you demonstrate passion for your idea, advice, or position on a matter. Overall, enthusiasm is a great asset in business. But if your enthusiasm runs high all the time, be on your guard. There may be certain situations that require a *lower* dosage. People whose enthusiasm runs on high all the time may be perceived as being insincere. Your listeners may feel you've thrown caution to the wind and haven't done all your homework. A good manager won't be fooled by unabashed enthusiasm for an idea that isn't backed up with hard data and facts.

TIPS FOR BUILDING YOUR ENTHUSIASM

1. Create enthusiasm by thinking enthusiasm.
We can psyche ourselves up by drawing upon our memories of when we felt enthusiastic. The fact that thoughts lead to feelings that lead to action guarantees it. This is valuable in many situations where a task lacks interest or challenge.

2. Know what you're "selling" and be prepared to sell it.
Whatever the situation you are facing, note the benefits of addressing it (for you and others involved) and envision how you will implement your approach. By virtue of your awareness of the benefits to be gained and the confidence that comes with thorough preparation, your level of enthusiasm is likely to be at its peak.

3. Introduce some fun or competition into the task that you are unenthusiastic about.
This will help get your mind off some of the drudgery and boredom that accompany certain tasks. A friend of mine runs a telemarketing department of about fifteen reps. Anyone who has ever done telemarketing knows what drudgery it can be. Wanting to juice things up a bit, he placed a bell on each employee's desk. Every time a telemarketer hit a particular sales milestone, he or she would ring the bell. Everyone really bought into the idea—it was fun, and it became very competitive in a positive way. Everyone wanted to be the first to ring the bell. It was also a public acknowledgment that someone was achieving the level of success set for the department.

4. Develop an attitude of gratitude.
To be genuinely enthusiastic, one must have a deep appreciation for life in general. Too often we take our health, loved ones, success, and other positive aspects of our lives for granted and focus almost exclusively on the things we struggle with. Too often we worry about issues that are really insignificant, and it drains our enthusiasm for life. Take a few moments to put your life into perspective. There are many people on this planet who would gladly trade places with you. Consider all that you have to be thankful for.

Your Uplifting Power is always available. Drawing on it will help you get through the bumps and bad breaks we all encounter.

9

Driving Power

Driving Power is the power to take bold, decisive action. Driving power requires determination, courage, and confidence. These are the "big three" traits involved in getting things done. Without them, great plans remain just that—hopeful words on a piece of paper. Nothing gets done until we move into action. If we do not activate our Driving Power, we run the risk of either never getting off the dime or giving up once the road gets a little rough. Let's take a look at the first of our Driving Powers, determination.

DRIVING POWER: DETERMINATION

Determination is defined as the tireless pursuit of a goal, purpose, or cause.

The word "determination" derives from the Latin word *determinare*, which means "to settle conclusively."

We demonstrate determination each time we . . .

- Find ways to get around barriers that stop or delay our efforts.
- Prepare a plan to accomplish objectives or complete a project.
- Stay committed to finishing what we've started, even if our time and/or resources run out.
- Refuse to admit defeat or inability to handle a challenge.
- Do not rely on the efforts of others.
- Are motivated by activities or goals that seem out of reach or impossible.
- Are self-motivated.

Nothing in the world can take the place of persistence. Talent will not; nothing is more common than unsuccessful men with talent. Genius will not; the world is full of educated derelicts. Persistence and determination alone are omnipotent.
— CALVIN COOLIDGE

THE LINK BETWEEN MOTIVATION AND DETERMINATION

Determination is fueled by motivation; the two are inextricably linked. You will not be determined unless you are motivated. Determination is being motivated to plan and persevere in order to meet goals, produce results, and improve continuously. When you are determined to meet a goal or improve your work performance, it's because you feel internally propelled by some type of force.

When faced with a mountain I WILL NOT QUIT. I will keep on climbing until I climb over, find a pass through, tunnel underneath, or simply stay and turn the mountain into a gold mine, with God's help.
— THE POSSIBILITY THINKER'S CREED

FINDING YOUR MOTIVATOR

Motivation arises from an emotion or desire that impacts your will, causing you to act in a certain way. Motivating forces can be either internally or externally generated. If you are motivated by an incentive, which is an *external* factor, you are probably inspired by a reward, such as a prize, a bonus, or a company-paid trip. On the other hand, if you are motivated by praise, which is an *internal* factor, you are probably inspired by a reward such as public acknowledgment for a job well done. The psychologist Abraham H. Maslow argued that people are motivated by and reach fulfillment through satisfying a series of needs. He described a hierarchy beginning with physiological needs, such as hunger and thirst. Once the basic physiological needs are met, Maslow maintained, we are motivated by the needs for safety, belonging, love, esteem, and self-actualization (the full expression of the individual).

Each of us has a set of motivating factors, some of which must be present in order for motivation to be intrinsic. The following list may help you discover your personal motivating factors.

1. Think about a personal success or accomplishment in your work life. Below are some examples. Note which of them apply to you.
   - A promotion
   - Being selected for a special task or project
   - Finishing an assignment
   - Serving on a team
   - Getting a raise
   - Doing a good deed for others
   - Coming up with a new idea
   - Learning a new skill
   - Recognition from others for a job well done
   - Other (list other events or experiences you felt good about)
2. Compare your list to the motivating factors below. Your primary motivators are the factors that you listed with the greatest frequency.

Section I

1. I was able to do what I wanted and thrived on the autonomy.
2. I provided love, caring, or help.
3. I felt as if I "belonged."
4. I became more confident and competent.
5. I found the activity enjoyable and pleasurable.
6. I learned or tried something new.
7. I was stimulated to meet a challenge.
8. I applied my skills and knowledge.
9. I developed my appreciation of life.
10. I stretched my capabilities and further developed my potential.

Section II

11. I received money, reward, or incentive.
12. I influenced others and held some power.
13. I met the expectations of a customer or client.

14. I received love, acceptance, caring, or help.
15. I did it with or for family and friends.
16. I received respect, attention, or appreciation.
17. I earned recognition, status, or prestige.

You're probably wondering what all this means to you. A primary motivator is a "payoff" factor. It's what you get from a situation or experience that makes you regard it with satisfaction or a feeling of success or achievement.

Your primary motivators may vary from one area of your life to another. For instance, the way in which you are motivated in friendships may differ significantly from what motivates you on the job. Are your two highest ranked factors from Section I or Section II, or is there one in each section? The factors listed in Section I are internal validations. These are motivating factors in which *you alone are the primary definer of your satisfaction, success, and achievement.* These motivators are rooted in your emotions, feelings, and learning experiences. If most of your check marks are within the factors of Section I, it means that you are motivated primarily by internal forces such as your own thoughts, beliefs, and affirmations. On the other hand, the Section II factors represent external validations. These are the factors in which *other people and external stimuli are the primary motivators of your satisfaction, success, and achievement.* If most of your check marks are within the factors of Section II, it means that you are primarily motivated by other people and their actions toward you.

Now let's determine which of the projects or activities provided you with the most motivational satisfaction. You can determine this by thinking about which activity stimulated the most motivational factors. The one that did tapped into several of your key motivators and fulfilled your needs. You'll probably find that the activities that were the most challenging for you were also the most rewarding.

CAPITALIZING ON YOUR MOTIVATING FACTORS

You can use the results of this survey in several ways. First, when you are faced with a choice of projects or tasks at work, you can target the ones in which your key motivating factors will be present. When you can match the opportunities contained in a project to your motivational "hot buttons," your level of determination in seeing the activity through will be optimized.

For instance, if you've identified that autonomous activities and learning a new skill are two key motivators, you would probably opt to be involved in a software training project rather than in a team project involving redesigning administrative forms. If you are having motivational problems when it comes to a certain work activity or project, you can reflect on the factors that are important to you and seek (or try to create) similar opportunities. Let's say that your supervisor has asked you to participate on a cross-functional team to research and develop a new service for your customers. The meetings you've had to date have been pretty boring, and you haven't engaged mentally in the project yet. You know that recognition and appreciation are your vital catalysts, so when the team seeks someone to fill the role of team leader, you volunteer for the position. In this role, you know that you can have these needs met because your responsibilities will include reporting your progress to the heads of both R and D and new-business development.

YOUR ROLE IN FOSTERING DETERMINATION IN OTHERS

If you supervise others, you can help them leverage their motivational interests and needs by encouraging them to seek out endeavors that truly mesh with their personal motivating factors. For instance, if you witness an employee being very enthused and motivated by developing customer relationships and making sure that customers' expectations are met, you should channel his or her energies into efforts that incorporate significant customer contact because that's where he or she will realize the most payoffs. When employees are responsible for activities and projects that do not fulfill their motivational desires, they may feel apathetic or lethargic. Over time, if people are loaded down with tasks that don't hit the motivational mark, their morale may drop noticeably. In today's booming economy with low unemployment and fierce competition for good talent, it is more critical than ever to find the motivators required to retain good talent. If you've ever been involved in a project or activity where you felt bored, depressed, or negative, there's a pretty good chance that it was due to a poor match of your motivational needs with those inherent in the project.

A STORY ABOUT DETERMINATION

Although women had been practicing law in the United States for 112 years before one was appointed to the Supreme Court, it took President Ronald Reagan only six days after meeting Sandra Day O'Connor in 1981 to nominate her for the highest court in the land. O'Connor grew up during the Great Depression on a vast ranch covering three hundred square miles in Arizona and New Mexico. After attending boarding school in El Paso, she went on to Stanford, where it took her just six years to earn both her undergraduate and law degrees. Although she was editor of the *Stanford Law Review* and graduated third in her class, O'Connor found no takers when she began applying for jobs with top law firms on the West Coast; the only position she was offered was as a legal secretary. But that didn't diminish her determination. O'Connor took the reins herself; she hung out her own shingle for a few years and then moved into public-service law. Her first position was as Arizona's assistant attorney general from 1965 to 1969. She was then appointed to the Arizona State Senate, to which she was reelected twice. A few years later, she became the majority leader of the Republican-dominated state senate, the first woman ever to hold that post. Two years afterward, she was elected as a superior court judge, and in 1979 she was appointed to the state appeals court.

Describing her level of determination, her sister Ann Day explained, "Sandra believes there is no problem for which she can't find a solution." Not only did her determination play a major role in her career, it also carried her through a major health crisis. In the mid-1980s, O'Connor was diagnosed with breast cancer and endured a mastectomy without even telling her siblings until it was over. She scheduled her chemotherapy sessions on Fridays so that the weakness and nausea that followed wouldn't keep her away from work. Her determination was the force that propelled her all the way from her rural ranch environment to the U.S. Supreme Court.

The Greatest Positive Motivator

We know that motivation is the key to determination. The greatest motivator is really intrinsic. That means that the desire to go on, even against all odds, comes from a place deep within us. I believe that place is what Maslow referred to as "self-actualization." I interpret self-actualization as the most honest, pure, unselfish expression of self. The motivator is our desire to achieve our greatest human potential through unselfish service to others. I view this as a *spiritually driven* motivator. The other motivators in Maslow's hierarchy are driven more by what we need for *physical and emotional survival.*

The greatest negative motivator is fear, which unfortunately motivates many people. (I'll talk more about it in the "Courage" section of this chapter.) Nothing fuels determination more than dedication to a cause.

The Consequences of *Too Much* Determination

The result of too little determination is clear: we give up and don't finish what we started. But what are the effects of applying too much determination?

Can there be a downside? I think back to a "fast-track" marketing executive who, in his determination and zeal to make a mark for himself and the company he worked for, left a trail of bruised and battered psyches along the way. He was a very driven individual with big ideas that he wanted to implement with instant results. His determination translated into a stubborn refusal to accept or even entertain alternative ideas from others in the company. Determined people often forget to employ patience. They can't seem to wait for other people to catch up with them, and their journey becomes a selfish pursuit of personal gain and glory.

I want to be careful not to send the wrong message here, because *almost always*, it's too soon to quit! Many of us give up just short of victory, and determination fueled by a sincere desire and interest to help oneself, others, and one's company is healthy and positive. All my professional life, I have striven to be motivated by a desire to contribute to the betterment of individuals and society as a whole. I am also a very determined person. There have been several times in my professional life when I have unfortunately allowed my determination to get the better of me, regardless of my positive motives and intentions. Often we get so caught up in the pursuit that we fail to recognize the warning signs that indicate we have drifted off course. It's important to watch for those signs.

How Do We Know When to Quit?

There's a simple, yet effective three-point checklist that can help determine whether or not we should abandon or redirect our pursuit:

1. When there has been a realignment of organizational goals and objectives.

We often fall in love with certain projects that capture our imagination and challenge us. For many reasons, there are times when we have to relinquish our control over them or abandon them completely. We must recognize that although we may have invested a lot of time and energy in a certain project, it is in the best interest of our organization to move on to the next one. In order to bring closure to the project, it may be best for you to assist in the transition and make sure you receive acknowledgment for your contributions.

2. When the cost exceeds the benefit.

Sometimes we cross a threshold at which the costs of an endeavor exceed both the short- and long-term benefits. We sometimes ignore or are not even aware that we have crossed such a threshold.

3. When the impact on our personal or professional relationships is negative.

Whether in personal relationships or professional ones, when others begin to suffer as a result of our determination, it may be time to give something up. For instance, if you have a spouse and children, going for a promotion by working eighty hours a week will probably have a negative impact on your home life. Professionally, pushing your coworkers, associates, or employees too hard will alienate them from you. Sometimes you can minimize or remove the negative impact altogether by openly and honestly discussing your reasons for driving so hard. Also, by showing more tolerance of and patience to those whose support you are counting on, you give them time to absorb and process what's going on.

Some people think that it's holding on that makes one strong.
Other times it's letting go.

— Anonymous

Tips for Building Your Determination

1. Remember your goal.
Goals and deadlines are great motivators. For example, while writing this book, I had deadlines for submitting various drafts to my publisher. I also have annual personal fitness and health goals that I set that keep me motivated. They become the extra push I need, for instance, to leave the warmth and comfort of bed on a cold, dark New England winter's morning to run six miles!

2. Attack doubt as soon as it creeps in.
Doubt is an enemy of determination. It sucks the determination right out of us and makes our spirit sag. Doubt usually consists of distortions and even lies that emanate from the subconscious mind. The source of this type of doubt is our self-limiting beliefs appearing in the form of negative self-talk, which we discussed earlier. Shakespeare wrote that our doubts are traitors because they unjustly sabotage our efforts. Attack doubt with positive, rational thinking, and it will vanish.

3. Focus on the benefits of attaining your objective(s).
Motivation comes from what you (and others) stand to gain from an activity. The more valuable the potential benefits, the greater your motivation will be. And the greater your motivation, the more likely you will be able to remain determined to accomplish your objective.

4. Know that your situation is not so unusual.
Most human stories have been enacted previously. Someone, somewhere, at some point in time has been faced with a similar, if not the identical, difficult situation that you are facing. So keep in mind that,

like others before you, you can gain victory by finding a way out, up, or through it all.

> *Genius is 1 percent inspiration and 99 percent perspiration.*
> —ATTRIBUTED TO THOMAS EDISON

DRIVING POWER: COURAGE

Courage is the willingness to take risks and overcome fears, even when the outcome is uncertain.

It's easy to be courageous when we know an outcome will be positive. It's easy to tell the boss what we think of his ideas if we know we won't lose our job as a result. Taking risks and bold, decisive action without knowing what the outcome will be, however, is true courage. If you've ever wondered why you often see a heart symbol associated with courage, it's because the word is derived from the Latin word *cor*, meaning "heart."

We demonstrate courage each time we . . .

- Dare to do things or take on tasks that seem formidable or impossible.
- Maintain a steady disposition in the face of danger, challenge, or crisis.
- Keep up group morale even when we're opposed or threatened.
- Express our thoughts about a controversial issue.
- Draw attention to injustice, even though it may be culturally accepted.
- Take a risk even when the outcome is uncertain.
- Adhere to our personal beliefs in the face of great pressure.
- Challenge the status quo if warranted.

Now, that's a tall order! But bringing our dreams and plans into reality often requires an enormous amount of courage.

THE POWER OF FEAR IN BUSINESS

Too little courage makes a coward. Remember the Cowardly Lion in the movie *The Wizard of Oz*? He was on a journey to the wizard to receive courage. "How can you be the king of the jungle if you don't have courage?" he asked his traveling companions. He was a cowardly lion because he feared *everything*. The word "coward" is derived from the Latin word *cauda*, which means "tail," as in when a dog runs away with its tail between its legs. Courage turned upside down is fear, and fear is what often prevents us from acting courageously in the workplace.

A friend of mine, Professor James Stoner of Fordham University's Graduate School of Business, once made a comment regarding fear in the workplace that has stuck with me for many years. We were actually talking about ethics in business and what motivates people to be unethical. His theory was that most unethical actions that take place in business are the result of a specific type of fear: the fear of not having enough money or not having any at all.

There are many good managers and employees who would never dream of committing an unethical act under normal circumstances. But for instance, if not hiding a mistake meant possibly losing one's job, an individual might choose to hide it. The fear of losing one's means of support has led many people astray. Professor Stoner made that point to me and added a helpful admonishment: "Always make sure you have some money tucked away so that you never have to make an ethical decision based on this type of fear."

A number of years ago, when I was working as a quality consultant, I was called into a company to discuss the possibility of installing a continuous quality improvement program. The company was a manufacturer of electrical equipment. As I was taking a tour of the plant, I asked the quality manager why there was suddenly an urgency to implement a quality program. He explained that until recently, the company had thought it had things under control relative to the quality of its goods. "Our quality reports never indicated that there were any problems," he said. "Customer satisfaction was high, returns were low, and internal scrap and rework were also low. Then one day, just a few months ago, there was a fire in one of our large garbage bins. When the fire department arrived, it had to forcibly open the bin, which is usually sealed. When they opened it, to our astonishment, it was packed high with scrap and other product not fit for use. We never knew what went in the bins because they were sealed until the disposal company carted them away." According to my host, he said that management had discovered afterward that the practice of hiding scrap and rework had been going on for years. No one had wanted to admit to the actual high levels of poor quality.

Fear creates a certain degree of desperation that can cause us to compromise ourselves. Many people mistakenly believe that courage is the absence of fear, but, to the contrary, courage is acting *in spite of* our fears.

A few years ago there was a story in *The New York Times* about a young man who dived off the Throgs Neck Bridge to rescue a young woman who had jumped off the bridge in an attempt to kill herself. For those of you not familiar with the bridge, it is one of the longest and highest in the New York metropolitan area. When the young man hit the water, he was knocked unconscious by the impact. Luckily, he and the young woman were saved by a rescue team. The media held him up as a fearless hero, someone willing to risk his life to save another. During an interview, he was asked how he had mustered up the nerve to jump off the bridge. "Weren't you scared?" asked the reporter. "Of course I was," he replied, "but I couldn't let her drown. I knew I had to do something." He acted regardless of the intense fear he felt.

If you must feel comfortable before taking action, you may never take the kinds of risks needed to accomplish your objective. It's OK to feel apprehension—even fear—before taking action. Fear is common among police officers and firefighters, but they are courageous because they act *in spite of it*. Courage is a necessary ingredient for their success, just as it is essential to yours.

COURAGE ON THE JOB

Every one of us has displayed courage at some time or another. Think about the most courageous thing you have ever done. Did it involve a physical risk? An emotional risk? A mental risk? A financial risk?

It might be helpful to ask yourself these questions: What made the situation one in which you needed courage? What were your fears? What were the uncertainties surrounding the situation? What gave you the courage to plunge ahead? Was it perhaps one of the following?

- I didn't have a choice.
- I developed a plan of attack.
- The potential payoff was greater than the potential cost.
- I believed in my ability to succeed.
- I was encouraged by others.
- I knew it was the right thing to do.
- Other reasons.

Looking back, how do you feel now about what you did? Do you feel happy, proud, sorry, relieved? Did you take an unnecessary chance? What role did fear and uncertainty play in your experience? How did others respond?

THE RELATIONSHIP BETWEEN COURAGE AND RISK

Courage is a very personal, subjective trait. What is risk taking for one person may not be for another. Courage is having the state of mind or spirit to face danger, fear, or unexpected changes with self-possession, confidence, and resolution. Courage involves the willingness to take risks. One of the greatest impediments to organizational change initiatives is fear. We don't want to venture outside our safety or comfort zone. But change is a part of life. It happens whether we like it or not and whether we are ready or not! With change come risk and continued uncertainty. Not long ago, I was asked to facilitate a change management program associated with the introduction of a new technology platform. Processes had been redesigned, requiring new procedures and policies. Not only would people have to do their work differently, they would also have to shift from a manual system to an automated one. There was fierce resistance to the changes. My first task was to determine the nature of the resistance. After conducting numerous interviews, I reached the conclusion that the resistance was due to fear and apprehension. Of course, no one admitted to that publicly; the fact emerged during continued probing. I remember vividly a comment made by a manager who had been with the company for many years: "I'm an old dog. I don't understand all this new technology, and besides, we've gotten along just fine without it all these years."

His fear and unwillingness to take risks were based on a combination of three factors:

- Fear of failure: we may not succeed.
- Fear of disapproval from others: others may not like what we're doing or may try to stop us.
- Fear of the unknown: we don't know the results of taking action in advance.

Courage is resistance to fear, mastery of fear, not absence of fear.
— MARK TWAIN

As you now know, courage is the willingness to face and/or overcome these three fears. There are several ways of doing this:

TIPS FOR BUILDING YOUR COURAGE

1. Identify and remove negative, self-limiting beliefs about the situation.
Fear, in most instances, stands for False Evidence Appearing Real. Perhaps the most challenging situation you are preparing for is somewhat fear-provoking. Realistically, what is the worst thing that is likely to happen? Chances are that it's hardly a life-or-death situation. Most of our worst fears are in our mind. Remember the famous words of Franklin D. Roosevelt: "The only thing we have to fear is fear itself."

2. Capitalize on your belief, integrity, and confidence.
People with strong beliefs, convictions, and confidence in themselves and what they're doing rarely have a problem acting courageously when a situation warrants it.

3. Conduct a SWOT analysis.
There will be some occasions (hopefully few and far between) where the risks are great and fear is difficult to overcome. In such situations, the SWOT (Strengths, Weaknesses, Opportunities, and Threats) Analysis Tool will help you to analyze risks objectively by maximizing benefits and minimizing costs. The result is an easier path to thinking and acting courageously.

Once you've identified a particular situation that requires courage, conduct a SWOT analysis by following these steps:

1. Identify your **strengths.**
   • What skills, experiences, attitudes, or beliefs do you have that will help you meet this challenge?
2. Identify your **weaknesses.**
   • What skills do you lack?
   • What negative beliefs or attitudes might get in your way?
3. Identify your **opportunities.**
   • What are the personal payoffs for meeting this challenge?
   • Why is this important to you?
4. Identify **threats.**
   • What's the worst thing that could happen?
   • What do I have to lose?

EXAMPLES OF WORK-RELATED ISSUES REQUIRING COURAGE

Here are some common work-related fears that might benefit from a SWOT analysis.

• Speaking up to superiors (upward feedback)
• Speaking up to peers in a group when your ideas differ from theirs
• Taking on a highly visible new project
• Taking on work for which you are unsure you have the skills (from either a content standpoint or a management standpoint)
• Making a job or career change
• Letting go of a project or work; having faith that others can do it
• Sharing power/control with subordinates and/or coworkers
• Giving constructive feedback to others

Now, where will you find the courage to face your fears and take action? Here are a few ideas:

• Develop a plan.
• Think about your past successes.
• Imagine the best outcome.
• Believe in yourself.
• Get support and encouragement from others.

- Learn and practice in a safe environment.
- Write a positive affirmation to change your self-talk.

Do you live adventurously, or do you hug the shore? I am not talking about taking foolish risks that could harm you or others. Courage without some degree of caution is nothing more than recklessness. All successful businesspeople have had to overcome their fears and take calculated risks. The best way to overcome our fears is to face them directly and take bold, decisive action. The more we practice courage, the easier it will become and the more our fears will diminish.

DRIVING POWER: CONFIDENCE

Confidence is being personally assured of one's abilities, capabilities, and potential.

One of the greatest maladies in business is lack of confidence. This manifests itself in low self-esteem, inferiority, and poor self-image. The word "confidence" comes from the Latin word *confidere*, meaning "to trust in someone."

We demonstrate confidence each time we . . .

- Do not let mistakes or failures erode our self-image.
- Do not fear being measured against others' expectations.
- Act with easy coolness and freedom from uncertainty and embarrassment.
- Act decisively.
- Hold nothing back in our quest for what we desire.
- Believe we have the knowledge, intuition, abilities, and know-how to complete projects competently.
- Are quick to volunteer ideas and suggestions.

Lack of confidence often stems from events that occurred early in our childhood. According to a research report that appeared in *Newsweek*, numerous scientific studies confirm what wise parents have long known: kids need lots of time and attention. The following is an excerpt from the report: "Studies have shown that babies who are hugged often and feel loved and cared for are much more likely to grow up confident and optimistic." As a youngster, you undoubtedly heard one of these two phrases: "You can do it" or "You can't do it." Either consciously or subconsciously, these old "recorded messages" probably still affect your self-image and confidence. Lack of time, attention, and positive reinforcement from significant adults early in our childhood can lead to a belief that we are not capable of performing certain tasks or taking on challenges. We convince ourselves that we do not possess the requisite talent, skill, resources, or experience. But since we cannot relive and redo our childhood, we must learn to let go of the past and explore ways of building our levels of confidence.

CONFIDENCE: YOU KNOW IT WHEN YOU SEE IT

Have you ever seen someone and thought to yourself, "That person sure looks confident"? What is it that makes us draw that conclusion about a person?

When you have confidence, it emanates through the way you carry yourself and how you shake a person's hand, look people in the eye, and speak.

Lack of confidence is also easy to detect, since it manifests itself in the same behavioral ways. In business, the greatest liability associated with lack of confidence is timidity. A timid person comes across as feeble, weak, and nonassertive. Lack of confidence leads to a downward spiral of negative thoughts and emotions:

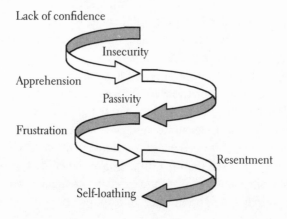

This downward spiral can cause people to avoid taking risks and to seek excessive and unnecessary reassurance. It can cause them to lack initiative, second-guess themselves and others, and be influenced easily.

These behaviors have a negative impact on workplace performance. They are responsible for secondary behaviors as well. For instance, people who have a tendency to second-guess their own decisions and actions are likely to cover their tracks in the event that something goes awry. They make sure they have a contingency plan designed either to shift blame or to provide ready-made excuses. In addition, an unconfident manager is likely to accept credit for other people's ideas and accomplishments.

A person who lacks confidence also tends to be easily influenced by the opinions of others. People with a low amount of confidence give in easily when faced with opposition or differing ideas. For instance, they may be easily influenced by others with "better" credentials: "She's got an MBA from Harvard, so she must be right." People with a low confidence level often seek approval from others before acting. In all likelihood, without approval they will not act. Seeking approval is not always a bad idea, especially when attempting something new or risky, but it is a crippling mistake to base all our decisions and actions on the approval of others.

OVERCONFIDENCE IN THE WORKPLACE

There is also, of course, a downside to having or exhibiting too much confidence, as this can be perceived as egotistical or arrogant. Overconfident managers are not likely to seek the ideas and opinions of others; more often, they are noncollaborative "Lone Ranger" types who seek their own glory and recognition. Sometimes the excessive outward display of confidence masks a deep-seated insecurity and fears. It reminds me of the "great and powerful Wizard of Oz" who, in the movie of the same name, appears as a loud, demanding, intimidating image before Dorothy and the rest of her group. Later, though, during one of his tirades, which has the main characters shaking in their shoes, the dog Toto pulls open a curtain concealing a control booth, revealing a timid, kindly, old gentleman. It turns out that the wizard's supposed power was only a facade.

THE "PERFECT" LEVEL OF CONFIDENCE

A healthy amount of confidence involves having a realistic, humble view of one's abilities, capabilities, and potential. The operative word here is "humble." The word "humility" comes from the Latin *humus*, or "ground." We can also take this to mean being in a "low place." Some people believe that humility is a negative trait and look contemptuously on humility as a sign of weakness. Wiser people recognize the grace and dignity of humility and honor it for its lack of arrogance. As the great Indian leader Jawaharlal Nehru once said, "Let us be a little humble; let us think that the truth may not perhaps be entirely with us." In that respect, humility involves knowing the truth about oneself and reflects an accurate assessment of one's abilities, capabilities, and potential.

Let's say you're a manager who has asked for a volunteer from your staff to lead a special task force. Which of the three following responses seems to suggest a healthy dose of confidence? Which shows a lack of it? Which seems to overdo it?

- "I'd like to lead the task force. I've participated before on a task force similar to this one with great results. I am experienced and knowledgeable. Although I have never led a task force before, I believe I can learn from others and do a great job."
- "I'm going to run this task force. No one else is capable. I'm the only one around here who can get the job done."
- "I think I might be able to do this. I kind of know what I'm doing. But I may need some time to think about it. What do you think? Do you think I can do it?"

Which volunteer would *you* select? The first response is closest to an ideal level of confidence. The second comes across as arrogant and self-centered. The individual may indeed be able to get the job done but may cause problems with other members of the task force. The third response is weak and noncommittal. The person seems to want someone else to make the decision for him.

How can you develop confidence? No one can give you confidence; it is generated from within. Confidence is driven by several primary factors:

- Self-talk: what we tell ourselves regarding our abilities, capabilities, and potential
- Level of experience: whether we have done something before, how many times, and with what results
- Past successes: the greater the success, the greater the confidence
- Reinforcement from others: encouragement, guidance, and positive feedback

The last item is an indirect driver of confidence. It is true that no one can give you confidence, but other people can facilitate your rediscovery of it.

TIPS FOR BUILDING YOUR CONFIDENCE

1. Acquire the required knowledge and skills.

When NFL Coach Bill Parcells took over the last-place New York Jets in 1997, he was quoted as saying that the first order of business was to build up the team's confidence. At the time, Parcells eschewed motivational speeches and pep rallies. He believed that the players had to start with a mastery of the basics: blocking and tackling. The Jets went from a one-and-sixteen team to playoff contender in one year. Learning the basics and putting in lots of practice time is the first priority in building confidence. Getting the basics down leads to victories, first small ones, then great ones. Nothing builds confidence like winning.

2. Use confident language.

Eliminate self-sabotaging, negative self-talk. Regularly use positive affirmations regarding your abilities, capabilities, and potential. Consciously eliminate negative phrases such as "I can't," "I'm afraid that . . . ," "That's impossible," "I could never do that, I'm just a lowly [fill in the blank]," and so on. These phrases are overgeneralizations, predict a negative outcome, and dismiss or ignore the possibilities.

3. Practice confident behavior.

Apply the "act as if" technique, even if you're not feeling confident. But "act as if" only if you genuinely do have the required knowledge and skills or are willing to learn them along the way. Body language is an important transmitter of confidence. Stand (or sit) straight and tall, look directly at the person you're speaking to, and speak with a steady, even, resolute tone.

4. Focus on your past successes, not your failures and mistakes.

It's sad how we take our successes for granted and dwell on our failures. If we obsess on failure, we tend to generate more failure. Instead, focus on your past successes. Ask yourself, "What factors led to success in each instance? What can I apply in the next situation?" It's amazing how many of us, when asked to reflect on a particular accomplishment, will talk about all the things that went wrong along the way. We tend to focus on the negative aspects *even if we were successful!* Sometimes we do make mistakes, and sometimes we fail. This can lead to a terrible feeling of unworthiness and low confidence.

There was a manager who, upon making an extremely costly mistake, acknowledged his error, went into his manager's office, and said, "I'm sure that after what I did you're going to fire me. I'll save you the trouble by resigning immediately." The manager responded by saying, "I do not accept your resignation. Do you think I'm going to let you go after making a million-dollar investment in your education?" The manager knew that it had been an honest mistake, committed by a dedicated, hardworking employee. The manager viewed this as a learning opportunity for a valued member of his management team. Too often, we expect immediate success in everything we set out to do. When we make a mistake, we blow it all out of proportion. Everybody makes mistakes, and *honest mistakes are nothing to be ashamed of.* The more we accept ourselves and others as fallible human beings, the easier it becomes to embrace our mistakes as valuable feedback or learning opportunities and keep them separate from our opinions of ourselves (and others). A former colleague of mine had a favorite saying that would help get her past a mistake: "God gave us tomorrow to make up for our mistakes from yesterday." I've found it to be a nice reminder to not dwell in the past, rather, keep our eyes fixed on a new day and another chance to "get it right."

5. Engage in preparation and practice.

Sometimes developing confidence is nothing more than being fully prepared. This includes rehearsal and practice to hone your skills, anticipate glitches, and work out bugs. It also means that you are equipped with facts or know how and where to find them. Whenever I give a speech, conduct a workshop, or make a presentation, I make sure I arrive well before the event to check my equipment, notes, data, and facts, the room setup, and so on. I leave nothing to chance or luck; there's no better "luck" than good preparation.

6. Seek out help and advice from others.

As we have seen, confidence is very closely linked with the "belief" trait. And belief, we learned, involves trusting in oneself, others, and/or a higher spiritual power to provide support and guidance when needed. This suggests that to build confidence, one should rely on one's belief to the fullest. It also suggests that others can help build our confidence by reminding us of our abilities, capabilities, and potential. Sometimes we lack confidence because we don't realize how truly gifted we are. If you are a manager, you have a responsibility and obligation to help others become aware of their talents and strengths. We should always be looking for ways of providing positive reinforcement to encourage and perpetuate confidence.

There is a great passage in Eleanor Porter's novel *Pollyanna* that underscores this point: "What men and women need is encouragement. Their natural resisting powers should be strengthened not weakened. . . . Instead of always harping on a man's faults, tell him of his virtues. Try to pull him out of his rut of bad habits. Hold up to him his better self, his *real* self that can dare and do and win out! . . . The influence of a beautiful, helpful, hopeful character is contagious, and may revolutionize a whole town. . . . People radiate what is in their minds and in their heart. If a man feels kindly and obliging, his neighbors will feel that way, too, before long. But if he scolds, and scowls and criticizes—his neighbors will return scowl for scowl, and add interest! . . . When you look for the bad, expecting it, you will get it. When you *know* you will find the good—you will get that."

There are other ways of rediscovering and reactivating the confidence within us. As one who believes in a God, I often turn to Scripture to remind myself that I am created in His image. And although I may not have all the necessary material resources, I have been endowed by the Creator with all the intangible raw materials necessary to gaining success in my endeavors. Whatever *your* source, it can be extremely helpful to seek encouragement from others and to be reminded that you are a person of tremendous worth and potential. Too often we lose sight of that simple, yet profound fact.

Your driving power is most essential in getting through the *day-to-day* struggles and challenges we face that can derail our best efforts.

10

Holding Power

No one likes to wait. Not you. Not I. *Nobody.* In American business, it seems as though speed is the order of the day: get things done, and get them done *fast!* Although I realize that the idea of "holding" runs counter to our frantic, warp-speed culture, if it is used at the right time with the right people under the right circumstances, it can make all the difference between successful and unsuccessful outcomes in our personal and professional lives. Holding Power involves employing the last (but certainly not least) of the ten traits of a positive thinker: patience and calmness. Of the ten traits, these are the ones that people consistently have the most problem activating and applying in business. At a glance it is easy to bundle patience and calmness together. This is because our common sense tells us to: when we're impatient, we become nervous and anxious. Likewise, when we are in a frenzied state of mind, we become much less patient with other people and circumstances. Hence, it would appear that patience and calmness are a package deal and therefore should be addressed as a whole. But upon closer examination, we see that there are subtle differences between them that warrant a separate discussion of each.

HOLDING POWER: PATIENCE

Patience is the willingness to wait for opportunity, readiness, or results from oneself and others.

I remember being surprised when I read the Latin source of the word "patience": *pati,* meaning "to suffer." At first they didn't seem to connect. But gradually I realized that patience does involve suffering, not necessarily in the sense of physical pain but rather in terms of the mental anguish we sometimes experience when forced to wait for an extended period of time.

We demonstrate patience each time we . . .

- Maintain our poise in a crisis.
- Wait calmly for events to occur and opportunities to arise.
- Use the passage of time to our advantage.
- Make a conscious decision to respond to a waiting period with an even disposition.
- Do not respond impulsively when forced to wait.
- Refuse to accept a less-than-desirable resolution of an issue simply to be done with it.
- Allow circumstances, relationships, and alliances to unfold naturally over time.
- Allow others to complete tasks according to their personal timing whenever possible.

Many companies, especially those in the service industries, have developed clever ways of preventing customers from becoming impatient. For example, mirrors are placed near elevators in hotels to provide a distraction for guests while they wait, music or taped messages are played while customers are on hold on the telephone, some restaurants supply games and gadgets to keep patrons busy while their meals are being cooked, and so forth. In today's society we are not very good at waiting patiently for anything.

That would lead many to think that *impatience* is more of the natural order. Patience is treated as a virtue that one is either graced with or not. But look at the definition of patience again—the first four words are "the willingness to wait." This suggests the notion of time and, more specifically, the *passage* of time. Think about that. There is a natural sense of timing associated with all living things. It takes nine months for a baby to develop in its mother's womb before it can be born. It takes several days for a seed to sprout. An inanimate natural wonder such as the Grand Canyon took millions of years to form into the exquisite beauty that it is. One of the reasons I like living in New England so much is because of the distinct change in seasons.

The seasons change right on cue, just as they always have. The natural rhythm expressed by the change of seasons supports the idea that patience is something that is built into nature. If anything, impatience is more of a learned behavior, driven by how we see others reacting to situations involving waiting.

Just yesterday I was driving with my two children, Jennifer and Andrew. We were stopped at a traffic light for what seemed to be a very long time. When the light turned green and the car in front did not move immediately, Jennifer said, "C'mon, Daddy, why don't you beep your horn to get them moving?" I thought back to all the times I had beeped at slowpokes on the road or muttered unpleasant things about them, never realizing that my kids were taking it all in!

Impatience is a selfish emotion whose possessor thinks that he is the center of the universe. It is driven in part by a need for instant gratification, which is reinforced by a number of factors. Technology, for instance, has made it possible to make purchases at a "click of the mouse." Faxes, e-mail, express service, pagers, and cell phones allow us to communicate with people anywhere in the world, at any time, very quickly, and that capability reinforces our impatience.

THE NEGATIVE EFFECTS OF IMPATIENCE IN THE WORKPLACE

Many problems arise as a result of impatience in the work environment. Impatient managers place undue stress and pressure on employees. They often do not take the time to listen to ideas or work through problems. In my experience as a quality consultant, I have seen quality problems go unchecked for years because managers did not have the patience to solve problems methodically. Instead, they would apply a "Band-Aid" for a quick fix. I am not suggesting that managers operate without a sense of urgency. There are dangers to waiting too long or having too much patience—we may miss an opportunity.

But consider how many poor decisions are made as a direct result of impatience. Or how many sales opportunities are missed when a salesperson tries to push a customer or prospect into making a purchase decision. Customers who feel pressured will sometimes back away, even if they prefer your product. One of the most important skills of a successful sales professional is having a keen sense of timing: knowing when to approach a prospect, place a follow-up call, ask for an order, and so on.

PATIENCE AND CHANGE MANAGEMENT

Managers often make the mistake of ignoring the natural rhythm that is inherent in all people during times of change. A few years ago, one of my clients decided to update and improve its computer systems. This involved massive changes to work processes, procedures, and policies. The resulting chaos affected everyone in the company, as well as its customers, and had an impact on everything from how customers placed their orders to how they paid for them. Here's what happened.

Having invested hundreds of thousands of dollars and being convinced that everyone in the company would welcome the changes, senior management decided to speed up the technology rollout by setting an arbitrary date of "the end of the year." Although I was not involved with the technology rollout, the senior vice president of human resources sensed that the implementation date was too soon and asked for my advice. I suggested that the implementation should be pushed back at least six months. I felt that more time was needed for the employees to understand and absorb all the changes. I also had concerns that their customers' potential reactions to the changes were not being considered. Management thought that because the technology would make life easier for customers, it wasn't necessary to consult with them. But there was no dissuading management, and the implementation took place on time, requiring the employees to use new equipment and follow new, more complex procedures. Unfortunately, the worst-case scenario occurred: the employees revolted, the customers went berserk! They jammed the phone lines, canceling orders, registering complaints, and expressing their dissatisfaction. "Why weren't we told about this sooner? You should have given us more time!" was the typical message. Their rebellion was not only loud but expensive. Management immediately applied the brakes on the rollout. They reversed course and extended the time frame. The rollout eventually did occur, but not without a lot of unnecessary grief and expense.

SITUATIONAL PATIENCE

When it comes to patience, some people run low most of the time, but for the vast majority of us, our patience levels have more to do with specific circumstances and people. They are also shaped by our particular mood or temperament at a given time. If you were to evaluate your patience levels on a daily basis and from situation to situation, you would probably see quite a bit of variation. Consider following three situations and imagine how your own patience level would be affected—and why.

Scenario 1

During the past six months, your company has been reorganizing, which has resulted in a series of layoffs. Your manager has assured you that your position is safe, but others who have been laid off were also given that same assurance. You have heard rumors that your department may be left intact but moved to another state. A more recent rumor is that your manager will be moved to a new location and you will become the new department head at the old location. You have been unable to verify either rumor. Your coworkers are restless and anxious. You love your position, but your spouse has indicated that he or she will not consider a move. If you become the new department head, you are worried about staffing because the best people in your department are considering looking for positions elsewhere.

Scenario 2

You're the manager of a major new development project with high visibility throughout your organization. If it succeeds, you will receive a substantial bonus. Although you have developed a schedule of all the deliverables, your manager continues to hound you about delivery dates. In addition, two key pieces of equipment you need to develop the project are now about two weeks late.

Twice the vendor has promised delivery "tomorrow," but you have yet to receive anything. You are experiencing problems with the development team as well. Two members appear to be completely disorganized. Although they are good workers, whenever you ask for a status report, they shuffle through papers and invariably say they will have to get back to you, although they usually do so within a day. Three other team members appear to have lackadaisical attitudes regarding the importance of the project. Another critical team member will be out on maternity leave for the next several months.

Scenario 3

Several months ago, you discussed your career objectives with your manager, who has served as a friend and mentor during the two years you have worked for him. As a result of your meeting, your manager asked you to put together a detailed plan outlining your goals and objectives for the next three years. You spent a lot of time on the plan and delivered it to him a month ago. Since that time, you have asked for feedback on several occasions, but the manager has continued to put you off, giving vague reasons for his inability to review your plan. This morning, when you approached him again, he became agitated and told you he'd get to it in due time.

If you were the person in the scenarios described, what would *your* level of patience be? If you found yourself reacting very impatiently, how would you have behaved? Perhaps you might have pushed harder or maybe made a hasty decision. I am not suggesting that you should not take action. Sometimes we confuse patience with inaction. For instance, in the third scenario, you would be justified in taking immediate action to find out what is going on. But because impatience can create so many negative emotions (see "The Three Enemies of Impatience," below), you would want to be sure to be extra cautious when confronting your manager to avoid having the negative emotions get in the way of a productive discussion.

> *Through patience a ruler can be persuaded,*
> *and a gentle tongue can break a bone.*
> —PROVERBS 25:15

THE THREE ENEMIES OF PATIENCE

Extreme impatience creates negative thoughts, which in turn create negative emotions and feelings. Three specific negative emotions surface as a result of impatience:

Frustration

This emotion can cloud your judgment and stifle your creativity because it inhibits your ability to think clearly.

Discouragement

When we feel discouraged, we literally "lose heart" (look closely at the word "discourage"; in it is another word, "courage," which, you may recall is derived from the Latin word meaning "heart"). We tend to throw in the towel and give up too easily—which, of course, affects the level of another one of our ten traits, determination.

Anger

This is the final, most destructive enemy of patience. When you are angry, you tend to overreact, hit the panic button, and lose your cool.

When you experience any of these emotions, you also tend to have physical reactions. Physicians tell us that emotions related to impatience disturb the rhythmic action of the small muscle fibers of the stomach and intestines. These emotions can also raise your heart rate and blood pressure. Each one of these emotions leads to negative actions, which, of course, lead to negative consequences.

I remember negotiating my first significant business deal. Because I knew I was inexperienced, I decided to seek help from an expert. I hired a lawyer friend who had considerable experience in negotiating deals to coach me through the process. I expected that the deal would take two to three weeks to complete and was anxious to get it done.

As the weeks stretched into months, I started to get impatient. In fact, I became so impatient that I wanted to settle after the first round of negotiations, as I felt that at that point the deal was fair. At the strong, calm urging of my mentor, I decided to wait longer. The process eventually took more than three months. But thanks to my mentor, the deal turned out to be significantly more lucrative for my company, as well as a fair deal for both parties. The greatest lesson I learned from the experience was the power of patience.

Decide that you will not try to do everything at once.
That is why time is spread out.
— DR. NORMAN VINCENT PEALE

PATIENCE BUILDS POWERFUL RELATIONSHIPS

There is a children's story about trust, friendship, and patience called *The Little Prince,* by Antoine de Saint-Exupéry. Although written for children, the book is packed with powerful lessons for adults; it has been a required book for the class I have taught at Fordham University's Graduate School of Business since 1993. The book features a young boy, the Little Prince, who leaves his small planet to explore other worlds. His travels bring him to Earth, where he meets a fox. He is intrigued by the fox because there are none where he comes from. Feeling lonely and unhappy, the Little Prince says to the fox, "Come and play with me, I am so unhappy." The fox explains to the Little Prince that he cannot play with him because he is not tame. The inquisitive prince asks the fox, "What does that mean—tame?" After the fox explains the meaning of the word "tame," the prince asks, "What must I do, to tame you?" The fox replies, "You must be very patient. First you will sit down at a little distance from me—like that—in the grass. I shall look at you out of the corner of my eye, and you will say nothing. Words are the source of misunderstandings. But you will sit a little closer to me, every day." As the days passed, the prince tamed the fox, and the two became very close.

The mind-set in business is very different. We pride ourselves on our ability to work quickly, effectively, and efficiently. We don't seem to have time to allow relationships to develop and grow. As a result, we build only superficial relationships. We mistake these superficial relationships for friendship. But building lasting relationships involves creating bonds of trust, and that takes time. All too often we look for the "quick hit" friendship: "Let me be your friend so I can get what I want. I will pretend to like you and be interested in you as long as you serve a useful purpose." We would do well to remember the story of the prince taming the fox, which provides a useful lesson about building powerful relationships.

IMPROVING OUR LEVEL OF PATIENCE

Almost all of the chronically impatient people I know view their impatience as a scourge that cannot be changed for the better. Their attitude is "Patience is a virtue that I have not been blessed with." There's hope, though, even for the "hopeless." The first step in becoming more patient is to isolate the specific reasons for your impatience.

SITUATIONAL IMPATIENCE

Consider the following list of common work-related situations that can create feelings of impatience. Do any of them try your patience on a regular basis?

- Time crunches; things not being done as quickly as you'd like
- Things not being done right the first time
- Not having the tools or information you need to complete a task
- Dealing with bureaucracy
- Others who don't have the skills to complete their assigned tasks
- Others who don't catch on quickly to what you want them to do
- Others who don't carry through on their assigned tasks
- Inconsistent messages from others
- Others who don't do tasks the way you would
- Too many people needing your time and attention
- Not enough time to do your work with real quality
- Last-minute crises or requests that totally upset your day or plans
- Having to wait for others
- Traffic, bad weather, broken equipment, or other inconveniences that delay your being productive or timely

By being more aware about the specific situations that create impatience, we can become more proactive in dealing with them. For example, we may become frustrated because others don't have the skills needed to complete assigned tasks. But instead of becoming impatient, we can try to suspend our impatience long enough to gather facts about the situation. We may discover that a person lacks a certain skill set because the training budget has been reduced or eliminated altogether. By keeping our patience in check, we can focus our energies on finding a solution to the problem.

In certain work-related situations that cause impatience, here are several far more general causes.

Fatigue
It's incredible how much lack of sleep can contribute to impatience. Fatigue saps us of the energy required to be patient.

Bias
Biases against others may make us less inclined to give them time and attention. Generally speaking, we tend to be more patient with people we like.

Lack of Interest
We may simply be uninterested in a topic or individual, creating anxiousness to move on to the next topic.

Ego
There are some people whose air of superiority or condecension is certain to try our patience. It is as if they are saying "What I have to say is important, what you have to say is unimportant. Therefore I really don't care what you have to say."

Poor Time Management
Procrastination and poor personal organization cause us to rush and to hurry those unfortunate enough to be in our path or dependent on us.

Illness
When we don't feel well, our threshold of impatience becomes very low.

Pressure
In today's work world, we are expected to do more with less at a quicker pace!

Personality
To the type A personality, *everything's* urgent and has to be done *now!*

• • •

Identifying the causes of *your* situational impatience is the first step in becoming a more patient person. Once you have isolated what you believe is a dominant cause, you can prepare a specific action plan to deal with it. For instance, if poor time management is your greatest problem, it would be wise to invest in literature and/or seminars to improve your time management skills. It's rare that you will find only one cause, but if you eliminate what you think is the greatest contributor, you will benefit quickly and then be able to turn your attention to the second greatest problem, and so on.

TIPS FOR BUILDING YOUR PATIENCE

1. Don't take delays personally.

Avoid negative self-talk. When waiting for someone or something, you may be tempted to think the worst: "The reason they're taking so long to get back with an answer on my proposal is that they've decided to go with another vendor" or "She hasn't gotten back to me on my staffing recommendations because she's upset with me about something." We all operate at different speeds. What you consider to be a reasonable time period may be totally unreasonable for someone else. If you are impatiently waiting for someone or something, ask yourself if the time it is taking is simply ridiculous. If it is, investigate the matter. If not, think of all the possible reasons there might be a delay. More than likely, you will begin to take the delay less personally and be able to cope with it more easily.

2. Distract yourself by keeping busy.

Waiting is difficult, especially when you're under pressure. A while back, I was called in to help a popular Boston-based retail store improve customer satisfaction. One of the key causes of dissatisfaction was the length of time customers had to wait in line when returning an item. The managers had been slightly taken aback by the news. They agreed that the lines were long but said that the average waiting time was only about four minutes. I decided to make a point about the relationship between waiting in line and customer satisfaction. I asked a group of the managers to close their eyes until I told them to open them. Then I let about a minute and a half go by. After they opened their eyes I ask them to guess how long they had been shut. Their responses were three minutes and higher. Time spent waiting always seems longer than it is. Then I asked them to imagine having two screaming kids at their side while they waited four minutes to return an item. That was enough for the managers. They agreed that they had to reduce the waiting time, as well as provide ways to make the actual waiting time *seem* like less.

Sometimes we have to distract ourselves simply by busying ourselves with other tasks. The mind can concentrate on only one thing at a time. For example, I've learned to take plenty of reading material along with me when I travel. With what seems to be more frequent travel delays, reading prevents me from dwelling on and feeling frustrated about something I have no control over.

3. Thoughtfully consider the consequences of acting now versus waiting.

Many times when we act impulsively, it feels good to have gotten an issue off our chests. But we may later discover that our quick action has actually complicated matters and compromised our position. Be sure to prepare a balance sheet on paper of the pluses and minuses of acting now instead of waiting.

In a recent edition of *Success* magazine, best-selling author and management guru Stephen R. Covey offers advice to proactive, action-oriented entrepreneurs who may tend to rush into situations without considering them carefully enough. Covey says, "Over the years, I've learned to use a simple technique to stay out of trouble. I'll count to 10—sometimes 50—when I have a new business idea or a strong creative impulse, to insert a brief pause between the stimulus and my response to it. During the counting, I'll ask myself, what is wise now? This basic technique helps restrain me from being over reactive or unwisely exuberant."

Whatever the reasons for our lack of impatience, with practice we can train ourselves to be more patient.

• • •

At the beginning of this chapter, I mentioned that the Holding Powers of patience and calmness are related, yet distinctly different. Many people have mastered the art of patience (at least outwardly), but internally they are in agony! Just because you're able to wait doesn't mean you'll feel good about it. Some people have to be patient whether they like it or not. Once I experienced a health problem with symptoms possibly associated with cancer. I went to my general practitioner, who immediately referred me to a specialist. Since it was a Friday, I had to wait through the weekend with the uncertainty. On Monday morning, I went to see the specialist, thinking that he would run some tests and make a diagnosis. Instead, he ordered more tests, which had to be performed by other specialists. I was dependent on their appointment schedule, which meant additional waiting time. Once the tests were done, they had to be reviewed and analyzed by the first specialist I had seen. It was agonizing. There was nothing I could do to speed up the process; I *had* to wait for things to unfold. Because the cause of my health problem was potentially life-threatening, I became increasingly anxious as each test was performed.

One day I decided to call my doctor to see if we could speed things up. But first I called my wife, Catherine, to ask her opinion (of the two of us, she's the levelheaded, "calm under pressure" one). I told her I was going to call the doctor and wanted to know what she thought. She said, "You only have six more days until your scheduled appointment. It will all be settled then, so a few days isn't going to make any difference. Just wait it out, and in the meantime try to relax." I was a little embarrassed because it occurred to me right then and there that I was practicing the "power of *negative* thinking." I had convinced myself that the test results would be bad. I decided at that point that I would be not only patient but *calm* through the entire process. I applied several positive thinking techniques discussed in this book, including positive self-talk and affirmations. I turned to my faith and found great comfort and solace. I even reread Dr. Peale's *The Power of Positive Thinking*. An overwhelming sense of surrender and peace came over me. The next six days passed quickly and calmly. The results of the tests were negative, and it turned out that there were no serious health concerns—other than the ones I had almost manufactured as a result of my obsessive worrying!

Another example that comes to mind in my professional experience has to do with the development of the "Power of Positive Thinking in Business" workshop. I had just left the comfort and security of my job at the Juran Institute because I had been asked by Peale Center management to write a business plan for the workshop. The funding for the project had already been approved, but management wanted to see the details. Some months later I submitted the plan and expected an immediate go-ahead. But instead I was told that the project had had to be put on hold. The Peale Center had just been merged into the much larger Guideposts Inc., which meant we would need approval from its CEO and management team. The Peale Center COO explained to me that we were now competing with other corporate projects with limited resources and that I'd have to wait for a decision from Corporate. He said it might take several months for the people there to sort through and prioritize the projects from both organizations.

This was a real letdown for me. I was anxious to get started because, after all, I had left my previous job to embark on this specific project. I thought, what if I wait this out and they decide not to go ahead with it? I was anxious to know the decision immediately because I didn't want to waste my time. But it was also clear that no amount of pressure would speed up the process since I knew that the CEO was a very thorough and methodical leader, who would wait until he had all the necessary information. I made the decision to wait for a response and, since I could not control the time frame, spent the time executing the parts of the project plan that did not require financial resources and subsequent approvals. During the waiting time, I was able to share the project plan with the Guideposts leaders, a move that turned out to be critical since they had not had input into the original idea. Taking the time to develop a detailed plan, and having the energy and patience to implement it, helped me build credibility and trust. I am convinced that had I pressured management before taking the time to build rapport with them, they might have rejected the project.

• • •

Now let's turn our attention to the much-desired, yet elusive Holding Power of calmness.

HOLDING POWER: CALMNESS

Calmness is maintaining serenity and seeking balance daily in response to difficulty, challenge, or crisis; taking time to reflect and think.

We demonstrate calmness each time we . . .

- Stop to think before acting.
- Consider what may be causing any feelings of tension.
- Balance the demands of work with the need to adequately address our physical, emotional, and spiritual needs.
- Maintain a relaxed disposition and a steady, rather than frenetic, pace.
- Are not overly worried or obsessed about a particular issue.
- Refuse to allow negative emotions to disrupt or control our frame of mind.
- Control our emotional responses.
- Take time out to regain or maintain our perspective on life.

Just saying the word "calmness" and repeating it in a soft, low voice tends to have a calming effect. Its root word evokes peaceful, relaxed thoughts and images as well. It derives from the Greek *kauma*, meaning "heat." It is said that people living in places with year-round warm, sunny climates such as southern California and Florida are more relaxed and easygoing.

Even if this turns out to be true, we can't all move to those places. The challenge is to learn how to become more relaxed and calm right where we are—no matter where.

When we are tense, irritated, and anxious, our emotions cloud our judgment. In his book *A Guide to Confident Living,* Dr. Peale points out that "A primary factor in tension is mental disorganization. The helter-skelter mind always feels overburdened. A disorderly mental state means confusion and, of course, tension. Such a mind rests lightly upon problems which it never decides. It skips nervously from one perceived problem to another, never arriving at a settled conclusion, in fact, not even grappling seriously with the issue involved. Thus deferred decisions accumulate. The result? The mind gives up and cries desperately, 'I am swamped'—simply because it is not organized. It is cluttered up and seems, therefore, to be overwhelmed. Note the emphasis, seems."

When we are relaxed and calm, it is easier to organize our minds. The result is a sense of power and control over ourselves. Our capacity for work increases, as does our pleasure in what we are doing. Strain and tension subside.

Edwin Markham, an American poet and author, observed, "At the heart of the cyclone tearing the sky is a place of central calm." The cyclone derives its power from a calm center. So do we. Out of relaxation comes a driving energy. Power is generated in and derived from a calm center. Angry, unchecked outbursts have derailed many a career over the years. No one likes working with a hothead. Sometimes it appears as if hotheads get away with their antics, but in the long run they come back to haunt them. The newspapers today are filled with stories about uncontrollable anger and rage being unleashed in violence on the highways, workplace, schools, sporting events, and malls. They appear to be reaching epidemic proportions. I don't know the reasons for it, and I don't think that most of us have the kind of explosive tempers that would make the headlines. But there is growing evidence that the stresses of contemporary life are causing even mild-mannered people to have more trouble keeping their negative emotions in check—all the more reason to develop the Holding Power of calmness.

> *The calm man, having learned how to govern himself, knows how to adapt himself to others; and they in turn reverence his (spiritual) strength, and feel that they can learn of him and rely upon him. The more tranquil a man becomes, the greater his success, his influence, his power for good.*
>
> —JAMES ALLEN, AUTHOR AND PHILOSOPHER

Think for a moment about your results from the Positive Thinking Inventory in Chapter 6. Where did you rank on the calmness scale? Now think about where on the continuum you *want to be most often.*

If you flip calmness over, you'll find a host of negative emotions: fear, anxiety, worry, tension . . . these emotions cause us to respond to life's challenges in an unsteady, frenetic manner. We then allow ourselves to be overwhelmed by concerns, resentments, annoyances, and irritations.

If you came up on the low end of the calmness scale, chances are that you're a worrier. Some worrying is warranted. In their book *Managing Your Mind*, Gillian Butler, Ph.D., and Tony Hope, M.D., argue that worry can have a good side if it serves any of the following three purposes.

- **As a danger signal:** Worry, in this case, alerts you to the fact that something is wrong. It is better to worry about customers' complaints than it is to dismiss them.
- **As an action trigger:** If worry compels you to take action, it's probably justified. For instance, going to the doctor to have a nagging cough checked out as opposed to ignoring it because you think it's "probably nothing" is a good idea.
- **As a coping rehearsal:** Worry can push you to take preemptive action, preparing you to cope. As an example, going to the doctor, as in the case above, might cause you to schedule regular annual checkups in the future.

But for the most part, worry is unhealthy and potentially destructive. It means "choking up." It wastes time and energy and interferes with your ability to concentrate. It leads to lack of sleep, nervousness, and anxiety. If it goes unchecked, it can cause serious physical problems. According to Butler and Hope, there are three things that, although they account for the vast majority of our worries, are not worth worrying about:

1. The unimportant. Most things that we worry about simply aren't worth it; they are too trivial. You have to ask yourself, "Do I *really* care about this? Will it matter twenty years from now?"

2. The unlikely. We worry about many things that never come to pass. We construct worst-case scenarios and convince ourselves that they're the way things will turn out.

3. The unresolved. "You never know until you know." Sometimes you just have to wait a situation out to the end. Circumstances can change unexpectedly and at any time.

If you came up on the low end of the calmness scale, chances are also that you experience stress most of the time. Experts have been telling us for years that a certain amount of stress is good for us. Stress is part of our instinct for survival; we can't live without it. Deadlines and other obligations and commitments create just the right amount of stress to propel us into action and get things done. But too much stress is *distress*, and that is harmful. The literature is overflowing with information on the damaging consequences of distress.

Tips for Building Your Calmness

1. Deal with problems directly and immediately.
Allowing problems to linger and fester erodes our center of calmness. Get into the practice of dealing with issues quickly, before they get out of hand.

Decide first whether or not a problem is within your control; if there's nothing you can do about it, drop it from your mind. If there is something you can do about it, try to deal with it one step at a time. Attempting to solve the "world hunger problem," for example, will crush and defeat you. There's an old riddle, "How do you eat an elephant? Cut it up into bite-sized pieces." Take a manageable piece of the problem and try to resolve *it* first. Then move on to the next issue. Ray Kroc, who built McDonald's into a multibillion-dollar hamburger chain, had this to say about dealing with problems: "I learned how to keep problems from crushing me. I refused to worry about more than one thing at a time, and I would not let useless fretting about a problem, no matter how important, keep me from sleeping."

2. Empty your mind of worry.
Practice emptying your mind of fears, hates, insecurities, regrets, and feelings of guilt. Imagine whatever is causing worry for you now fading from view, getting smaller and smaller until it disappears. (Merely making the effort will provide some relief.) Pour out to somebody you can trust those worrisome matters that occupy your thoughts, and by

doing so you will gain a more rational, objective perspective. Write your worries out on a piece of paper, and resolve to do something about the issue(s) prompting them at the appropriate time.

A friend of mine whose dad died a number of years ago told me that after all these years, he still held some anger and resentment toward him. His dad had been an alcoholic and had apparently made life miserable for the family. Wanting to put it all behind him, my friend sought help. He was advised to write a letter to his dad describing all his anger, hurt, frustration, and resentments, take it to his dad's grave site, and burn it. It had great symbolic meaning and significance for him: he vented his emotions, released them, forgave his dad, forgot about his resentment, and moved on.

This technique also works in reverse. That is, sometimes we need to seek forgiveness. Once when I was in college, I went on a weekend interfaith retreat sponsored by the Catholic Church. One evening we were assembled in a dimly lit room and discussed the power of seeking forgiveness for wrongs we might have committed over our lifetime. We were asked to privately write every wrong we could think of on a Post-it Note (some of us needed poster-sized Post-its!). When we were finished, we stuck the Post-it on a wooden cross, which symbolized unconditional love and forgiveness. Then, one by one, we removed our Post-its and burned them at the foot of the cross. Almost twenty years later, I can still remember the silence as we wrote everything out. And when the Post-its were all set ablaze, I can also hear the sniffling around the room and see the macho men trying to hide their eyes as boxes of tissues circulated around the room. A tremendous catharsis and healing took place; it was a powerful moment for everybody. This exercise can be transferred into the business setting with similar results—only instead of burning the sheets of paper, you could run them through a paper shredder.

3. Deal with physical symptoms of stress quickly.
Watch for the physical warning signs of stress. The first signs of losing your calm can be felt physically: pressure in your chest, trembling, tightness in the jaw and back of the neck, grinding teeth, and so on. Treating the physical symptoms quickly will prevent additional problems. Dramatic physical symptoms can very quickly become prob-

lems in themselves. You can usually manage physical symptoms by using simple breathing and relaxation techniques. Regular exercise is also an excellent way of dealing with physical symptoms.

4. Take advantage of your belief and focus traits.

Belief plays a powerful role in calmness. As a reminder, belief is trusting in oneself, others, and/or a higher spiritual power to provide support and guidance when needed. Sometimes consulting a trusted friend, adviser, mentor, or clergyman is all we need to get past tough situations that are disturbing our calm. Many people are afraid to ask for help; they view it as a sign of weakness. If you believe in a higher spiritual power, I suggest strengthening your relationship with it. For me, staying in touch with God through prayer, meditation, and Scripture reading has always been a sure way back to calmness.

Increasing your focus is also important. When you try to do too many things at once, you become unfocused and disorganized. As mentioned, a cluttered, disorganized mind leads to stress. Planning and prioritizing your work on a regular basis will give you a feeling of control that will lead to a clear, calm mind.

5. Control how you talk to yourself and others.

From the time you awaken in the morning, affirm peaceful, contented, and calm attitudes. It is important to eliminate all negative ideas from all of your conversations, since they tend to produce tension and internal stress. Remember, the words we speak have a definite effect on our thoughts, which affect our feelings and actions.

6. Work toward greater balance in your life.

Achieving balance in life can be difficult. If you're like most people, you probably find that giving attention to one aspect of your life—for example, your career—means sacrificing another aspect, such as your personal relationships (with your spouse, children, friends, and others). Balance in life is not a static concept. Rather, it is vibrant, dynamic, and always changing (sometimes unexpectedly).

The key is to become more aware of the important aspects of balance (spirituality, relationships, money, career, education, health, and so on) and prioritize them according to their relative importance in life. Once you create a prioritized list, you can easily assess and evaluate how you're *actually* living your life compared to how you *wish to* live your life and make the necessary corrections.

Holding Power requires tremendous discipline because it seems contrary to our notion of what is required for success: we link progress to action and speed. But Holding Power is equally important, and, when applied effectively, yields powerful results.

The heart of this book is the four powers of positive thinking: centering, uplifting, driving, and holding. By now you may be wondering "How am I ever supposed to remember everything—and, more important, apply it?" The answer is *practice, practice, practice*. In the Resource Section at the end of this book is a Professional Challenge Worksheet that provides a template for the systematic application of the positive thinking principles, techniques, and tools discussed in this book. I strongly suggest that you read this section carefully. The worksheet takes you through each step of the "Positive Thinking Road Map," which will serve as a guide to help you navigate your journey successfully. We have enjoyed enormous success with the many people who have attended our "Power of Positive Thinking in Business" workshops. I'd love to hear about your successes with positive thinking. Please feel free to share your experiences with me at sventrella@aol.com. You could also visit our Web site at *www.positivedynamics.com*. In the meantime, don't give up. With positive thinking, *anything* and *everything* are possible!

Resource: The Professional Challenge Worksheet

One of the best ways of achieving results after reading this book is to apply the concepts to an actual challenge, problem, or opportunity you are currently facing or expect to be faced with in the not-too-distant future. The Professional Challenge Worksheet is a tool designed to help you document and work through your particular problem or situation. The worksheet follows the sequence of the Positive Thinking Road Map, which you read about in Chapter 1. Whenever possible, by anticipating and documenting your situation *before* it occurs, you will be much better prepared to deal with it and thus more likely to achieve the desired result. It takes time and discipline to complete the worksheet, but eventually the steps may become so familiar that you can simply run through them in your mind, leading to the spontaneous application of positive thinking.

The following is an example of a completed professional challenge worksheet.

Professional Challenge Worksheet

1. What is the problem or situation you face?
I must present an update to management on my project in one week. The project is over budget and two weeks behind schedule.

2. What are you telling yourself about this problem?
- What events have led up to this problem?

The project team learned of an alternative solution requiring further analysis that drove the costs up and put us behind schedule. Management was not briefed on the change in status in a timely manner.

- **What are you telling yourself about this problem? (Your self-talk)**

I messed up big time. I can't be trusted to do the important jobs. I am irresponsible. I should have stuck with the original solution. I shouldn't have listened to my team members' suggestions.

- **Is what you're telling yourself in step with the world as it truly is or how you wish (or insist) it to be? (Your self-limiting beliefs)**

I beat up on myself pretty bad when things don't go as planned. I don't like to make mistakes—it makes me feel like a failure. I realize that's not true, though. In this particular situation things got off track, but for good reasons.

- **What is a more realistic, rational, constructive way in which you could view this event?**

It's true that we're behind schedule and over budget, but this new solution will ultimately save time and money and enable us to serve our customers better. We did the right thing for the company.

- **How can viewing the event in a more realistic, rational, constructive way benefit you and any others from the workplace who will be involved?**

It will help me focus my energy in a more constructive manner than finger-pointing. I will avoid becoming defensive during the management presentation.

- **How can you change your original self-talk to reflect your new perspective on the event?**

I'm a capable manager. I've led other projects that were very successful. Management knows that my track record has been very good. I've also gained valuable insights that will be helpful in future projects.

3. **What is your desired outcome?**
   - **Write a Specific, Measurable, Action-oriented, Realistic, Time-bound goal for this situation.**

Goal 1: Preserve management's support for the project
- Receive approval for additional funds (10% of original) within one week of the presentation.
- Receive approval for extending the completion date by one month.

Goal 2: Complete the revised project on time and on budget
- Provide final recommendations to management by December 31.
- Implement within budgetary parameters (10% of original).

- **Convert goals into affirmations. This is a goal stated as a *positive, personalized* statement that will fuel your goal attainment.**

Affirmation 1: Management's support is preserved for my project.
- I'm receiving the additional funding necessary to complete the project.
- I'm receiving approval for a time extension.

Affirmation 2: I am completing the revised project on time and on budget.
- I'm providing the final recommendation to management by December 31.
- The project is being implemented within the budgetary parameters.

4. Access your traits.

Focus (increase): Concentrate on the benefits of the new solution as opposed to apologizing for deviating from the original plan.

Calmness (increase): Some members of the management team may be upset. But don't lose your cool. Maintain a steady disposition, especially if you are under fire. Don't become defensive.

Enthusiasm (decrease): The perception by some will be that the team messed up. Overenthusiasm may lead some to believe that we are not concerned about time or budget.

Patience (increase): Management may need time to mull over their decision. Don't push too hard. Be willing to gather additional information to assist them with a timely decision.

5. Mentally rehearse the situation.

Visualize:

- Who is in attendance
- Where they will be seated
- Where I will be positioned
- What presentation equipment I will use
- How I will use the equipment
- How I will respond when being asked tough questions

6. Take action.

- Prepare presentation.
- Prepare handouts.
- Create agenda.
- Distribute agenda.
- Arrive thirty minutes early; check equipment.
- Distribute handouts prior to meeting.
- Handle questions after the presentation.
- Prepare meeting minutes.
- Distribute meeting minutes.
- Follow up with management.

7. Lessons Learned

(Note: This section is to be completed after an event—in this case a meeting—takes place.)

Although there was some initial tension, the meeting went well and the desired outcomes were achieved. In the future, I will be more diligent in providing written status reports to management *before* things get out of control.

I will also demonstrate greater confidence when reporting to management by having backup data readily available. By doing so, I will be better able to handle tough questions.

Acknowledgments

This book has evolved over a long period of time. I am grateful for the help I have received from many different quarters, in some cases before pages were ever written. Thanks to Jack Navarro, a genuine positive thinker who helps keep me true to the principles in this book; Professor Jim Stoner from Fordham University, for all his guidance and wise counsel; Professor Dave Fearon from Central Connecticut State University, for helping me refine my verbal and writing skills; Robert Reiss, for his inspiration, energy, and enthusiasm; Jim Andrews, Vince Daley, Joanne Dearcopp, Deborah Dowling, Dick Dunnington, Phil Fleming, the memory of Wendell Forbes, Jerry Hadley, Ed Newman, Arthur Pell, Dan Quinn, Frank Troha, and Michael Worfolk for providing insight and support; my literary agent, Patti DeMatteo, who believed in the book because she lives the principles; my Simon & Schuster editors, Fred Hills and Veera Hiranandani, for their patience, understanding, and excellent editorial suggestions; my assistants at Positive Dynamics, Stephanie Bent and Kirsten Richter, who kept the pressure on me to keep writing; Ruth Stafford Peale, who provided me with the privilege of developing the workshop and the book; Elizabeth Peale Allen, who as Peale Center manager and board member provided constant encouragement and direction; George Hart, who as archivist and chief historian gave me access to the materials and information necessary to write this book; Joan Alkiewicz, for her administrative support and moral support; Guideposts Inc. CEO John Temple and CFO Dave Teitler; Peggy

Cowherd from IBM Global Services; Mike Rodgers from Fort James Corporation; Mary Money from PepsiCola; Violet Vickery from Interstate Batteries; my friends and colleagues at the Juran Institute, especially Sally Archer, Brian Eck, Blan Godfrey, Laura Halloran, Karen King, and Bob Wilson.

And above all, thanks to my parents, who raised me to be a positive thinker; my siblings, who have provided support and encouragement over the years; and my in-laws, Fred and Madeleine Duerst, who provided counsel and guidance.

Index

About Positive Dynamics

Positive Dynamics is a performance consultancy specializing in the development and delivery of programs designed to help companies achieve unprecedented levels of performance by leveraging the inherent potential in people and work processes.

Positive Dynamics provides consulting, executive coaching, onsite workshops, train-the-trainer and keynotes based on *The Power of Positive Thinking in Business: Ten Traits for Maximum Results.*

Our programs and services are available in targeted formats, including:

- Leadership
- Change Management
- Sales
- Customer Service
- Teamwork
- Project Management
- Quality Improvement

For further information, contact:

POSITIVE DYNAMICS
26 Cricket Lane, Suite 5
Wilton, Connecticut 06897
203-563-0866
www.positivedynamics.com